Colvin's Clinic

Bonanza - Debonair - Baron
Maintenance Simplified

By
J. Norman Colvin

Published By
McCormick-Armstrong Co., Incorporated
Publishing Division
1501 East Douglas Ave., Wichita, Kansas 67201
Copyright 1984 By J. Norman Colvin

Library of Congress Card Catalog Number 84-60672
ISBN 0-911978-02-X

i

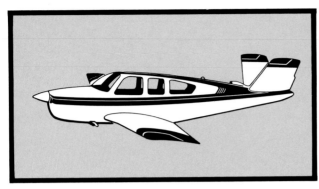

BONANZA V35B

BONANZA A36TC

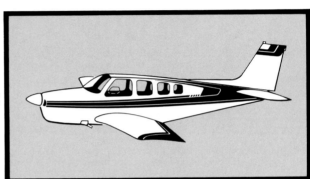

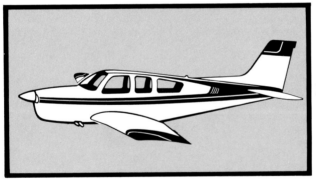

BONANZA F33A

BARON 58TC

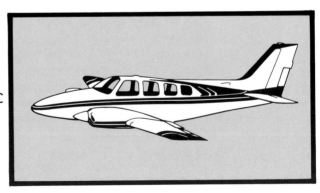

DEDICATION

This book *Colvin's Clinic,*
I have dedicated to YOU.
To Beech Aircraft Corporation
And those who've worked there, too.
To the American Bonanza Society.
To all its Members, past, present and those
to be.
To those Mechanics who've learned to love the
work they do.
And yes, to the Wives who occupy seat one
or two.
AND FINALLY
TO THE MOST BELOVED AIRPLANE that we
will ever see.
From the 35s, the 33s thru the B36 TC.

Nellie Colvin

J. Norman Colvin
50 Years In Aviation

ABOUT THE AUTHOR

After my retirement from Beech Aircraft Corporation in 1976, the American Bonanza Society asked me to serve as its Technical Consultant. I accepted in 1977 and am still enjoying that position.

In this book I have attempted to share, as much as I can, the knowledge I have gleaned in my years of work with this most loved of airplanes, the Beechcraft Bonanza. I hope this will be of significant practical help to the members of the Society and to others involved with the Bonanza.

Because it may be useful for readers to know something of my background in aviation and technical qualifications, I am including a summary of my fifty years of personal involvement with aircraft.

In 1934, I attended the Spartan School of Aeronautics in Tulsa, Oklahoma. Late that same year, I asked Walter Beech for a job as a welder; but I flunked the test. I returned for more schooling, then took a job with the Spartan Aircraft Factory as night watchman and worked up to foreman in the Sheet Metal Department making 55 cents an hour.

I met Nellie in Tulsa in 1936, and we were married in 1937. By 1938 I was an instructor at the Spartan School of Aeronautics, but later that year accepted a better job with Curtis-Wright in St. Louis, Missouri For the first time we had a bank account, so we thought life was great! But labor troubles arose. The plant went on strike and closed down March 1, 1939. A call to Beech Aircraft gave me the welcome news that I had a job whenever I could get there. On March 4th I was at work on the Model 18 fins in Wichita, Kansas. I later worked in the Final Assembly and Experimental Departments.

Early in 1941, just after the attack on Pearl Harbor, I took a leave of absence from Beech to help organize and teach in the National Defense Training School. Three months later Beech recalled me to work with the placement of the school's graduates. After the war, I worked briefly in Personnel, then transferred to the Service Department.

My first job in Service was handling warranty claims and conducting Service Clinic inspections. Then for eight years, traveling by car, I conducted Mobile Training Schools for Bonanza dealers' mechanics. When Beech introduced the Musketeer, I volunteered and was accepted as Project Service Engineer for this newest Beech plane. The project was moved to Liberal, Kansas. I went along, expecting to stay two weeks to help them get started, but couldn't get away for nine months. I was glad to stop commuting weekends, as Beech assigned me Project Service Engineer to the Bonanza and Baron series.

As a project engineer, my job was to listen to customer complaints, and shoot trouble by phone or letter on customers' airplanes; instigate service letters and work with the FAA on the need for AD's; work with engineering in resolving trouble in the product and suggest areas for product improvement; investigate trouble problems on customer airplanes in the field and investigate accidents on a limited basis; attend quality control meetings and quality spot checks of new airplanes on the final assembly production line; work closely with the experimental shop and flight line; conduct seminars and attend various conventions such as the American Bonanza Society, the Flying Dentists and the Flying Physicians. I conducted Service Seminars for the FAA and State Aviation Commissions. Along with these duties I was sent on two occasions to Colombia, South America, for the Beech T-34 training program.

One requirement was to always keep a suitcase packed. When I went to work in the morning, I never knew where I might be by night. As you can see, it was demanding but a fun job.

I obtained my pilot's license in 1945 and my A&P license in 1951. As a hobby, which has never ceased to be fun, I have bought and rebuilt wrecked airplanes.

It's my hope that this book will serve as a guide for correct maintenance of the Bonanza and will also serve as a useful segment of the total recorded history of this great, unique airplane.

Norman Colvin
January 1984

AUTHOR'S COMMENT AND CAUTION

The purpose of this book is to make the owner aware of maintenance problems that often are overlooked, as well as to make routine maintenance less of a chore. CAUTION: However, the author is unable and does not warrant the advice or his opinions contained herein to be applicable in each reader's situation or to his or her particular Bonanza maintenance or repair problem. Each person's fact situation necessarily will or may be different; and the advice and opinions contained herein might become obsolete and therefore should not be relied upon exclusively.

The author highly recommends that the reader's particular Bonanza maintenance or repair problem be referred to an authorized and certified aircraft and engine mechanic and/or aircraft inspector or authorized repair station.

It is also suggested that the selection of such professional persons be limited, if possible, to those who are familiar and experienced with the particular aircraft and engine model for which repairs or maintenance is sought. The use of the contents of this book, by the Bonanza owner, should be very helpful in conversing with and informing the professional mechanic of the nature of one's maintenance or repair problems and accomplishing the required fix.

Happy Flying

J. Norman Colvin

THE BEECH FACTORY AND YOU

Like most factories, the Beech Aircraft Corporation Factory has rules to protect both the factory and its dealer organization. While you may pick up your new airplane at the factory, you must buy it from an authorized Beech dealer.

At the factory, where you will be treated royally, you can select your interior fabrics and colors, exterior colors and paint design, and your avionics package. So, you see, Beech will truly build an airplane just for **you**. However, if you need a part for your airplane, you cannot buy it directly from the factory. It also must be purchased through the dealer organization.

Factory spare parts are stored in Salina, Kansas, 100 miles north of Wichita, and shipped from there to all distribution points. United Beechcraft in Wichita, a factory-owned distributorship, has an advantage over others in that they request a part to be picked up by a factory truck which delivers the part to the Wichita plant. United can drive across town to get the part, and it's on its way to you the same day.

While we tend to think of an airplane as being a 1960 or 1983 model, the factory identifies parts mainly by serial numbers. They have a good reason for doing it this way, since part changes occur at a given serial-numbered airplane, which might come off the production line at any time during the production year. So be sure you know your airplane's serial number, if you have an occasion to call the factory for information.

The factory does not release blueprints or other classified information. They will not approve any installation with used parts or parts from other vendors. However, the factory **will** honor other factory-installed vendor warranties that may exceed the Beech Factory warranties; and there are some Beech items, such as windshields (warranted for 5 years) that exceed normal factory warranty. When settling warranty claims, the factory folks and factory policies consider circumstances and past history of problems. In fact, as a whole, you will find the people and the Beech Factory good to deal with.

CONTENTS

Dedication..iii
About The Author ....v-vi
Author's Comment and Caution vii
Beech Factory and You viii
Inspections 1-2
Up-Grading Versus Up-Trading 2-3
How to Save Money...3
Selecting Paint Schemes 4
Buying a Previously Owned Airplane................................5-6
Engines 6-28
Cowl Flaps..29-30
278 Propeller 30-32
Fuel System...32-41
Heat and Vent System 42-45
Landing Gear System...46-68
Control Cables...69-70
Wings 71-79
Fuselage 80-85
Tail Section 86-89
Cabin Door 89-93
Skin Canning 94-95
Airframe Fatigue 95
Structural Integrity 95-96
Reskinning Control Surfaces...97
Magnetic Compass Deviation.......................................97
Brakes 97-99
Repair After Belly Landing 99-101
Case of Trouble..101
Trouble Shooting..102-113
What To Do...113-115
Odds and Ends...116-120
Notes From My Little Black Book 121-124
Service Clinic Inspection...125-133
Airplane Model Changes 134-140
Conclusion 141

TOPICAL INDEX

A   About The Author v
     A Case of Trouble - Next Case 101
     Airplane Model Changes
        Bonanza..134-138
        Debonair 138-140
     Air Frame Fatigue 95
     Alternate Air Doors...26-28
     Alternators 12
     Annual Inspection Costs 1
     Author's Comment and Caution vii

B   Beech Factory and You viii
     Belly Landing - Repair Afterwards 99-101
     Bonanza Brakes..97-99
     Break-in Procedures
        Steel Cylinders..6-7
        Chrome Cylinders 7-8
     Buying a Previously Owned Bonanza 5

C   Cabin Door 89-93
     Compass - Magnetic Deviation 97
     Conclusion 141
     Continental Fuel Injection...............................18-19
     Control Cables...69-70
     Control Surfaces - Reskinning 97
     Cowl Flaps...29
     Crankcase - IO-520 12

D   Dedication...iii
     Dzus Fasteners 80

E   Exhaust System...8-11
     Engine Cowling 84-86

F   Fairings - Rubber 79
     Fluctuating Fuel Pressure 25
     Fluctuating Fuel Pressure on a Cool Day 25-26
     Fuel Delivery Components Trouble Shooting
        Engine Driven Pump 19-20
        Trouble Shooting the System 21
        Trouble Shooting the Throttle Metering Valve 21-22
     Fuel Delivery Lines 22

F   (Continued)
     Fuel Flow Change After Engine Change 23
     Fuel Filter System 24
     Fuel Manifold Valve 22
          Trouble Shooting the Manifold Valve...................22
     Fuel Nozzle...................23
          Trouble Shooting Nozzles 24
     Fuel Tank System 32-41
     Fuel Transmitters 41-42
     Fuel Vapor...................24
     Fuselage...................80-83

G   Gap Strips 79
     Gust Locks 70

H   How To Save Money...................3
     High Oil Consumption 14-15
     Heat and Vent System 42-45
     Hot Starts 28

I   Idle Mixture 26
     Induction Air Filter 11-12
     Inspections
          100 Hour and Annual 1
          Walk Around Inspection 2
     Landing Gear
          Retract System...................49
          Actuator Rods 49-51
          Lift Legs...................52-53
          Gear Box and Motor 53-58
          Doors Hang Open...................58
     Landing Gear Motor 67
     Landing Gear Up Lock Block...................67-68

M   Main Gear Shock Struts 63-66
     Mud Scrapers 63
     Mufflers 114-115

N   Nose Gear
          Nose Gear Doors 46-47
          Nose Gear Struts 59-63
     Notes From My Little Black Book
          General Information 121
          Instrument Air...................121
          Adhesives 121
          Air Conditioners...................121
          Cowling 122

N (Continued)

Cabin Door..122
Electrical 122
Engine 123-124
Fuel 124

O Odds and Ends

Oil Filter 116
Converting From The Beech Electric Propeller 116
Ceveland Brake Mounting Flange Cracks 116
When You Install Cleveland Brakes...................................116
Water Will Accumulate In Hydraulic Brakes 116
The Flex Hose 116
Right Hand Fuel Tank Has A Leak 117
Fuel Delivery Lines...117
Landing Lights - V35A and V35B 117
Engine Driven Fuel Pumps 117
Popeller Overhaul 117
Oil Tank...118
"E" Series Engine Cylinders 118
Voltage Regulators For Generators...................................118
Fuel Gages V35 118
Controls Creep In Flight 118
Cleveland Brakes 119
Airplane Trim..119
Aileron Trimmer 119
Fuselage Covers..119-120
Early Turbocharged Bonanzas..120

Oil Consumption - High 14
Oil; Cooler 13

P Paint Schemes - Selecting...4-5
Poem - Conclusion..142
Propeller - Beech 278...30-32
Pumps - Vacuum...15-16
Pumps - Pressure 16-17

S Schematics

Exhaust System (Figure 1)..9
Pressure Pump (Figure 2) 17
Fuel Injection System (Figure 3-4) 18-20
Alternate Air Doors (Figure 5) 27
Cowl Flaps (Figure 6)...29
278 Propeller (Figure 7)..31
Fuel Systems (Figure 8-9-10) 33-36-38
Heat and Vent System (Figure 11-12)...........................43-45
Nose Gear Doors (Figure 13)...46

S (Continued)

Step (Figure 14) 48

Landing Gear Actuator Rods (Figure 15-16) 50-52

Landing Gear Motor (Figure 17)...............................54

Shimmy Dampner (Figure 18) 58

Nose Strut (Figure 19) 61

Main Gear Shock Strut (Figure 20)............................65

Landing Gear Up Lock Block (Figure 21)......................68

Wings (Figure 22)...71

Wing Flaps (Figure 23) 75

Fuselage (Figure 24)..81

Tail Section (Figure 25) 86

Cabin Door (Figure 26) 90

Service Clinic Inspection....................................125-133

Shimmy Dampner 58

Servicing Shimmy Dampner.................................59

Skin Canning...94-95

Stabilizers - G33 89

Step

Retractable 47

Fixed 47-48

Structural Integrity 95-96

T Tail Section 86-89

Tail Tie Down Ring..84

Trouble Shooting

Trouble With A Lesson To Be Learned 102

Erratic Fuel Gages V35......................................103

Air Static Check 103

Exhaust Valves...103

Light Or Heavy Crankase 103

Carburetor Engine Quits On Roll Out........................104

Fuel Injection Engine Quits On Roll Out 104

Oil On Rear Seat Carpet.....................................104

Gear Lube Comes Out Vent Hole In Gear Box 104

Airspeed Reads Erratic 104

After Landing, Main Gear Door Hangs Open 104

Prop Spinner Cracks..104

"E" Series Engine Won't Start 104

Throttle Or Mixture Control Creeps 104

Magnetic Compass Eratic...................................104

Low Manifold Pressure In Turbocharged Engine 104

Kit For Higher Emergency Landing Gear Extension 105

Excessive Uneven Main Gear Tire Wear 105

Erratic Fuel Gages In V35B Series 105

Fuel Siphons From Vent Tubes..............................105

Bottom Of Fuel Tank Lifts 105

T   (Continued)

Where Do You Lean The IO-470 & IO-520 Series 105
Cleaning Oil Tank and Radiator on "E" Series Engine 105
Things To Watch In Emergency Landing Gear System 106
Fuel Boost Pumps 106
Non-Congealing Oil Radiators 106
Uneven Fuel Flow From Auxillary Fuel Tanks....................106
After Prop Strike 106
When Voltage Regulator Quits On Early Series
      Bonanzas 107
Oil Drips From Induction Pipe Drain....................................107
Cabin Exaust Vent..107
Oil Temp Bulb In "E" Series Engine.....................................107
Improper Magneto Timing..108
Compass Deflection 108
Vibration...108
Generator Belts 108-109
Valve Lifters 109
Oil Leaks...109
Prop Spinners 109
Chrome Plated Spinners...110
Spinner Repair 110
Shower Of Sparks and Magnetos 110
Mounting Ailerons 111
Propeller and RPM Restrictions 111
Shortening Prop Blades..111
Rock Nicks In Prop Blades 111-112
Air Leaks In The Cabin 112
High Oil Consumption..112

Service Clinic Discrepencies and Their Fix
Fuel Siphons From Tanks..113
Cowl Flap Control Linkage Out of Rig 113
Cleveland Brakes 113

U   Up-Grading Versus Up-Trading 2-3

W   Wings...71-74
What To Do
Buying Another Engine 113-114
Worn Tires 114
The Hangar Door Blew In On My Bonanza 114
Vertical Scale Instruments..114
Taking Pictures From A Bonanza 114
Mufflers..114-115
What Happens When The Cabin Door Pops Open 115
Cowl Doors Pop Open 115
Medallions On Cowl Doors 115

W   (Continued)
    Walk Around Inspection 2
    Wing Flap 74-79

ANNUAL INSPECTION COSTS

If you have owned an airplane for any length of time, you have probably been hit at some time by a big annual repair bill. If your bills are regularly far lower than other owners' bills, then you probably are not getting good annuals. Bonanza annuals or 100-hour inspections should take from 19 to 21 man-hours to complete. This includes opening up the airplane by removing inspection plates, floorboards, wheels; running compression checks and so on. Any discrepancies found and repaired will be billed as extra charges. The flat rate time should include research for applicable Service Bulletins and AD compliance.

Sometimes the better Service Facilities are accused of "running up a big bill." Such accusations are more likely to be made by owners of airplanes that have previously received maintenance in a less qualified shop. Contrary to popular opinion, most service shops do not enjoy presenting you with a big bill. For this reason, during a Service Clinic, I find things that have been overlooked.

Just because it's a big, elaborate service shop, a small Beech dealer, a factory-owned or a privately owned shop, quality work is not always assured. The better shops employ a full-time inspector who inspects the opened-up airplane, writes up a "squawk-list," researches outstanding Service Bulletins and AD's, inspects the mechanics' work and completes the required paperwork. Chances are you will get a better job in this kind of shop, but there is no real guarantee. Some of the best maintained Bonanzas are maintained by their owners.

100-HOUR AND ANNUAL INSPECTIONS

When it comes time for your 100-hour or annual inspection, ask your Service facility how many man-hours they spend on the inspection portion only. The answer should be 19 to 21 man-hours. This is important since some shops spend as high as 40 man-hours while others may take only 10 or 12. So ask.

It is wise to occasionally take your airplane to a different shop, since a given shop may tend to get into a rut and may consistently overlook an important area. 1000 hour inspection periods are especially important since it is at this point special items such as flap actuators should be disassembled and greased. 2000 hours is another important time since it is at this point that items such as gearbox and shock struts should be rebuilt or replaced. Take your airplane to a major Beech shop at this time as they have the parts and equipment and know-how to do the job.

1

WALK-AROUND INSPECTION

Be a creature of habit when you do your walk-around inspection.

Start with the cockpit first. Remove the control lock if it is in place and check to see that all switches are off. Walk aft along the right side of the fuselage. Look at the static button in the side of the fuselage. Be sure the holes are open. If you have an emergency location transmitter, be sure it is armed. Remove the tail tie down rope. Check the elevator and rudder on the 33 and 36 Series and the ruddervators on the "V" tail for condition and security. Move them by hand. Look at the vertical fin side skins on the 33 and 36 Series for cracks just forward of the rear spar. Look at the fuselage skin above and below the stabilizer attach area for skin wrinkles. Look at the tail cone for obvious damage and especially the light lens. Work your way forward along the left aft fuselage. Look for obvious damage. Look at the static button for obstructions. Look at the left flap for damage. Move the left aileron up and down; look for free movement. Check top of wing for damage. Look for raised area above landing gear that would result from a broken uplock spring. Move on around the left wing. Flip the stall warning vane and look at the pitot tube. Untie the tie down rope. Check fuel level in wing; if equipped with tip tanks, check fuel level. Check bottom inboard wing area for fuel stains; drain the fuel sump in the wing and the sump in the fuselage. While bent down, glance at the fuel vent; it should point forward. Glance at the tire for inflation level and obvious damage. Look at the lower strut for obvious fluid leaks. Glance at the ramp or floor below the brake caliper for hydraulic leaks. Look at the left cowl flap for condition. Look at the nacelle side vents for undue residue. Check oil level. Check prop blades for condition, spinner for security and cracks.

Note cowl doors for security. Look at the nose tire for inflation and condition. Look at the nose strut for inflation and fluid leaks. Move on around to right hand engine nacelle, check cowl door for security and nacelle side vent for undue stains. Drain tank sump. While there, note fuel vent for position, tire for inflation, tire for condition, strut for (3") extension, strut for fluid leak, brake for hydraulic leak. Note forward wing root for fuel stains, lower and top wing for wrinkles and obvious damage; check fuel level. Move on around wing, look at tip for obvious damage or fluid level in tip tank; move aileron up and down. Look for freedom of movement. Then load baggage and personnel. When the last passenger steps on the step and the tail hits the ground, don't go or off-load baggage.

UP-GRADING VERSUS UP-TRADING

The Bonanza is probably the most modified airplane in the world. It is hard to look at two Bonanzas sitting on a ramp, side by side, and be certain what model they are. Kits provide extra windows, extended baggage doors, extended cabins, long slope windshields, new side windows with the new storm window, fresh air scoops, wing tips, new exhaust air vents, larger engines, heavier shock struts, new instrument panels and the list goes on.

Let's say you love your old G-model but you would like to have more speed and range. It is getting close to TBO, so should I dress the old girl up and install a newer, more powerful engine? Now, that third extended window kit is pretty, but it is expensive and it takes a lot of man-hours to install since it involves considerable structural part changes. The extended baggage compartment and added kit weight moves the CG further aft which makes a marginal aft CG problem worse. The long slope windshield will pick up airspeed; it is heavier and is ahead of CG which helps, but it should be done when the new instrument panel is installed. This alone is costly since this calls for considerable rewiring. It is always great to have more power, but horsepower must be squared for every mile an hour airspeed is increased. Horsepower does improve take-off and altitude performance, but the larger engines use more fuel. You reduce range, increase fuel costs and worst of all, it makes a morphodite out of your Bonanza because there are no charts or manuals that apply to your changed airplane.

Now there is something else to consider. Admittedly, Bonanzas look pretty much alike, but that is where the similarity ends. Changes were made structurally to each model. These changes are not readily apparent but they are there. While this extensive modification enhances the desire to own the airplane from a buyer's standpoint, it doesn't increase the value enough to offset the cost. In my opinion, you are better off to buy a later model that comes equipped with the features you want. You will buy a safer airplane with what you want for no more money.

HOW TO SAVE MONEY

As we all know, aircraft parts have long since passed the point that they are inexpensive. There are some factory-built parts that require tooling and should be supplied new by the factory. However, there are many other parts that you can build yourself or have some local shop build at a fraction of the cost. For example: the nose gear actuator rod boot. This boot attaches to the fuselage on one end and clamps to the actuator rod on the forward end. This boot is made of canvas and is all of ten inches long. There is no reason why you cannot remove the torn boot, take it to your local upholstery shop and have it duplicated. It might cost you $10.00 but it would be as good as the factory boot and would cost much less.

There are similar boots on the main gear actuator rods; some are made of chamois and others canvas. The uplock block uses a canvas boot and the wing flap actuator is protected by a canvas access cover. Any of these items can be locally made and be just as good.

Brake master cylinders need boots to prevent dirt from damaging "O" ring seals in the master cylinders. Make this boot from chamois skin and simply tie the skin around the master cylinder and master cylinder piston.

The windlace that prevents air noise around the cabin door can be easily made. Use the existing rubber and make the cover from naugahyde that comes in a multitude of colors. It can be purchased at most lady's fabric or upholstery shops. Many aircraft repair shops can make items such as brake hose. They buy the bulk hose and swage on the fittings. Aircraft upholstery is nothing more than automotive upholstery that is sprayed with fireproof material.

You can buy sheet aluminum to make skin repairs. The only real advantage to factory skins is that they have locating holes. When it comes time to overhaul, items such as fuel boost pumps, flap motors, landing gear motors, prop pitch change motors, electric prop governors, shock strut repair, fuel cell repair, new fuel tanks, aileron, flaps and ruddervator reskinning, call the American Bonanza Society headquarters. They have a list of good facilities that can repair and rebuild these costly items at a fraction of the new cost.

Your fuel tank leaks. Should it be repaired or replaced? Well, the least expensive way is to have your tank repaired. If the tank was built by Uniroyal, it most likely can be repaired. If the tank was built by Goodyear, chances are it cannot. A properly repaired tank should be quite satisfactory. It would be wise to get repair cost before sending the tank in for repair. American Bonanza Society headquarters lists several shops that build new tanks for considerably less than factory parts; a new tank would be better so compare prices and down time. If your tank is a 40 gal tank, ask if the new tank includes a baffle. It costs less without the baffle, but the baffle is an added safety factor.

SELECTING PAINT SCHEMES

When you decide to repaint your Bonanza, be original and sketch out your own design. The Beech Factory does not have patterns for a given model, they work from a sketch. The actual stripes are laid out freehand by the paint crew and of course, conform to the approved sketch. The more stripes and the more colors selected, the more masking tape and man-hours are required which relates to cost. It is best to paint the wing's leading edge white or a light color since the light colors reflect heat; it will keep fuel inside the wing cooler, which in turn lessens the chance for vapor. Paint adds considerable weight, so when repainting, be sure to remove the old paint. Most current paint is polyurethane and is stronger and heavier than enamel. It differs from enamels in that it is not porous, so if the skin is not properly prepared, filiform corrosion will develop. Filiform corrosion is a living fungus that will loosen paint and primer from the aircraft's skin. This causes the paint to wrinkle and eventually fall off. This condition can occur any place on the airframe surface, but is more prevalent at skin laps and around rivet heads. This condition caused the factory so much trouble that they now treat the skins before assembly. Then they electrostatic prime both surfaces with polyurethane primer so that filiform corrosion will not occur under skin laps or under rivet heads.

The skin surface should be treated with an alodyne solution to stop filiform corrosion, and, of course, skins must be dry before applying primer. Magnesium control surfaces should be stripped. The factory uses Paint-gon and then the surface is washed with Dowtreat and primed with a light coat of polyurethane primer. Control surfaces should be supported by the trailing edge so that any paint flow will aid in the balance process. Be stingy with the color coat. If the color and prime coats are too thick, the surface won't balance out and must be stripped and repainted. Ruddervators are more sensitive to balance than ailerons since they balance tail heavy, while ailerons balance nose heavy. Balance is an FAA requirement but some paint shops fail to comply, so check your log books for a compliance entry.

BUYING A PREVIOUSLY OWNED AIRPLANE

Buying a previously owned airplane is like buying a used car and can be a risk. The first rule is don't buy some freak, regardless of how good the price looks. By freaks, I mean airplanes like the twin engine "V" tail Bonanzas. Fortunately, not many were built; those that were had many bad faults. Beech built a series of Bonanzas with big engines and big generators, that were flown as drones. These planes were built for the military and somehow were made available to the civilian market. It would be most difficult to get such an airplane approved. Don't buy an airplane that is highly modified with kits whose builder has long been out of business. Don't buy anything that requires a blueprint or approval from Beech because release is against Beech policy. Log books can be deceptive. For example, they may say all AD's complied with, when in fact, none have been. The identification placard is the most valuable item on a totally wrecked Bonanza. A builder can assemble an airplane from salvage parts from a wide range of models, and rivet on the identification placard that shows model and serial number. This then makes the assembled airplane that model. Most owners are a breed apart. Many, for example, will have a low compression cylinder fixed before they will sell you their airplane. If the airframe is free of wrinkles and if the airplane flies out well, chances are it is a good airplane.

Two safe rules to follow. First write the FAA in Oklahoma City and pay someone to research the records. This will tell you the true history.

Then take it to a good Beech shop, and have the airplane placed on jacks. Partially retract the gear and look for worn landing gear and gear bushings. Retract the gear and listen for unusual noise in the gearbox. See that the landing gear doors close. Look for oil leaks, uneven tire wear, cracks in the crankcase. Look up the muffler tail pipes for worn or missing cones. Have someone research the log books and check to see that all AD's and Class One Bulletins have been complied with. If all this checks out, then go negotiate the price.

BREAK-IN PROCEDURE WITH STEEL CYLINDERS

"Good old Joe" is a fine mechanic and has been overhauling engines for years. Unless Joe has the proper equipment, such as a magna flux, ziglo or equipment to replace valve guides and seats, reamers and hones, plus equipment to rebuild starters, alternators, fuel pumps, oil pumps and vacuum or pressure pumps, Joe is not equipped. While he has been overhauling engines for years, he hasn't been doing a first rate job for years. Because an engine overhaul shop has the equipment, it doesn't necessarily mean that it can turn out a good engine. So be careful in your selection and talk to other owners who are flying their engine.

Correct break-in procedure is essential. Here is how it should be done:

Have the tachometer checked for accuracy before starting the newly overhauled engine. Using the airplane as test stand, **first run** should be made at no more than 900 RPM for a period of five minutes. Check all temperatures, oil and fuel pressures and check all engine accessories for proper operation. After initial run, allow engine to cool for six to eight hours. Overnight is preferred. During the cool-down period, check for oil leaks; check the engine compartment for controls' freedom of movement, travel limits and clearance. Check oil level.

Second run. Run engine ten minutes, not exceeding 1200 RPM. Check all engine instruments for correct reading and for operation of accessories, such as vacuum pumps, generators, etc. *Do not cycle propeller.* Allow engine to cool a minimum of 4 hours. Again check engine compartment and oil level.

Third run. Run engine for ten minutes, and not to exceed 1600 RPM. Check magnetos and cycle propeller. Idle engine, check for idle RPM. Turn both magnetos off momentarily to check for magneto ground. After engine has cooled, check oil level and bring to flight level.

Fourth run. Fly the airplane. Keep engine temperatures as cool as possible during taxi. When oil and cylinder heads are in operating range, advance throttle smoothly to full throttle take-off RPM. Note RPM for governor operation. Establish climb at 120 MPH, adjust cowl flaps half open. On the "E" Series engines, reduce power to 2300 RPM, 24 inches MP. Maintain these power settings in cruise and climb flight. Reduce power to 25 inches, 2500 RPM on IO-470 and IO-520 series engines. Continue climb at 120 MPH for 10 minutes at 25 inch MP if possible and lean to keep engine smooth.

Level off and reduce power to 24 inches MP and 2200 RPM, full throttle if 24 inch MP is not possible. Lean engine to peak EGT and enrich 25 degree below peak. If there is no EGT, lean until engine runs rough, then enrich mixture until engine runs smooth, then enrich one-quarter turn of vernier. Fly 30 minutes at these cruise settings. On descent, close cowl flaps and maintain 24 inches MP and 2200 RPM while descending to traffic altitude. Enrich mixture *gradually* during descent, *not all at once.* Fly normal pattern, full rich. On landing, in your post-flight inspection, check nacelle for discrepancies. Check oil consumption and bring it up to flight level.

Fifth and final run. Flight should be two to four hours with power settings 70 to 75% using 23 inch MP and 2300 RPM or 24 inch MP and 2400 RPM on the IO-470 or IO-520 Series. Keep cylinder head temperatures and oil temperatures and pressures normal. Oil consumption should stabilize somewhere between 25 and 50 hours. *Note:* Do not confuse this procedure with factory recommended procedure for their new or remanufactured engine.

ENGINE BREAK-IN PROCEDURE
WITH CHROME CYLINDERS

This procedure is for engines with fresh chromed cylinders using the aircraft as a run in test stand.

First run. Do not exceed 1000 RPM and only long enough to get oil and cylinder head temperatures to move. This does not mean that they reach the green arc. This should take five minutes or less. During this run, note other engine functions, such as oil pressure, fuel pressure, vacuum, generator and check magnetos, still at 1000 RPM. Check both magnetos to off, momentarily, to check ground. *Do not cycle propeller.* Stop engine with idle cut off and secure engine and airplane so that no one will turn propeller, not even 10 to 15 degrees. Let engine cool completely, five to six hours, preferably overnight. Check oil level and bring to flight level. Check nacelle for oil leaks, security and clearance of all controls.

Second run should be first flight. Get airborne as soon as temperatures are in the green. Taxi time should do this, still do not exceed 1200 RPM. **Do not cycle propeller.** Make a normal full throttle take off by advancing throttle smoothly. Check for rated RPM for governor operation. Establish 120 MPH climb and when at a safe altitude, reduce power to 25 inches and 2500 RPM, 2300-24 inch MP on "E" Series engine; close cowl flaps and lean the engine slightly.

On climb out, monitor cylinder head temperatures closely. Raise cylinder head temperatures to 410⁰ F (210⁰ C) reading. It may be necessary to lean slightly in the climb. Reduce RPM to 2300 while maintaining 25 inch MP and monitor cylinder head temperatures as they rise. If necessary, slow the airplane by raising the nose to increase cylinder head temperature.

As cylinder head temperature continues to rise, the oil temperature will also increase, the oil pressure may drop slightly, but this is normal. Hold cylinder head temperatures at 410⁰ F for about two minutes. Level off and reduce power to 24 inch MP and 2200 RPM. Start descent at once, maintain 24 inch MP and descend 300 to 400 feet per minute. As you descend, cylinder heads and oil temperatures will cool slowly to normal. **Note:** as you descend, gradually enrich mixture (but not all at once). Use normal approach and landing pattern approach speed and full rich.

Post-flight inspection. Look for oil leaks, oil level, oil screens and engine nacelle for discrepancies.

Next flight should be two to four hours with power settings of 24 inch and 2200 RPM or some similar settings.

After approximately ten hours, at the above power setting and when oil consumption has stabilized, return to your normal operating practices.

Regardless of engine type, oil consumption should not be over one quart for every five to ten hours of operation. Use mineral base oil during break-in period, then switch to ashless dispersant type oils or Phillips XC or Shell W oil.

Note: This engine break-in or run-in schedule is not to be confused with factory recommended procedure for their new or remanufactured engines or engines in new aircraft.

EXHAUST SYSTEM

There is more to the exhaust system than meets the eye. For example, the manifold is formed in two pieces from stainless steel sheets. The two pieces are heliarc welded and then the mounting flanges and ball slip joints are added. The completed manifold is placed in a large oven where all oxygen is removed from the oven. The oven is heated to 1700⁰ F where the part is allowed to heat soak for a period of time. After soaking, the oven and part are cooled by nitrogen. This process normalizes the part, removing internal stress that would cause cracks in service. The muffler and muffler-heater are built by Hanlin Wilson, a highly respected builder of aircraft exhaust systems. The exhaust tail pipes are Beech built.

The ball joint built on the exhaust manifold (Fig. 1-1) allows the manifold to shift or move independently of the muffler. The ball joints

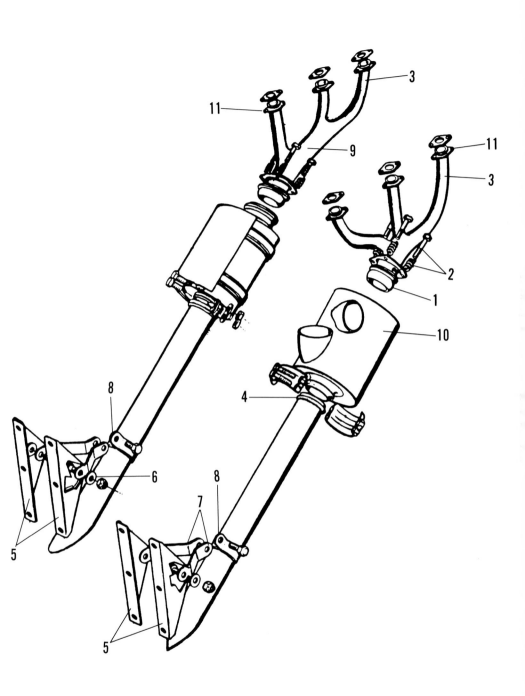

**Exhaust System
Figure 1**

on the manifold and muffler are held in place by a collar that is held in place by spring-loaded bolts (Fig. 1-2). These ball joints are inclined to leak exhaust gases which exit the nacelle side plates. We need some flexibility in the joint; otherwise, the front exhaust stack at #5 and #6 cylinder (Fig. 1-3) may crack. A similar slip joint is provided at the aft end of the muffler. Exhaust gas leaks can be cut down at this joint, by applying two wraps of stainless steel safety wire around the joint and tightening the collar.

The exhaust tail pipe was extended to exit below the fuselage. This did quiet the cabin some. The tail pipe is supported by two brackets per stack (Fig. 1-5). These brackets rivet to the firewall. Steel clips attach to the support bracket and the mounting is cushioned by two rubber grommets (Fig. 1-6) in the bracket (Fig. 1-7). The two steel clips attach to the clamp around the exhaust tail pipe. The exhaust tail pipe should clear the fuselage keel by about one-half inch. This clearance can be adjusted by moving clamp (Fig. 1-8) up or down the exhaust tail pipe. The size and shape of the exhaust system has been calibrated to give the least amount of back pressure. Adding additional mufflers to the exhaust tail pipe upsets the efficiency of the exhaust system. They also add weight to the tail pipe—weight that the tail pipe support bracket was not designed to carry.

The EGT probe should mount in the exhaust manifold below #2 and #4 exhaust stacks (Fig. 1-9). A cracked exhaust can be welded but only with heliarc.

Look for lead residue around exhaust gaskets and on adjacent engine induction pipes. Look for lead residue from below the muffler shell (Fig. 1-10). This would indicate a cracked muffler. Both mufflers have what are called flame cones built inside the muffler. Flame cones quiet the exhaust and in the case of the heater, direct hot gases to the heater case. Flame cones will burn out or crack loose from the muffler. They can cause severe engine back pressure. New cones can be installed reasonably so, if needed, contact American Bonanza Society headquarters for the vendor's address.

Exhaust mounting gaskets can and do give trouble. The steel mounting flange (Fig. 1-11) on the exhaust stack warps which presents a crooked base for the gasket to seal. The only way to correct this situation is to remove the manifold, place it on a surface plate and straighten the flange. Sometimes, when engine cylinders are reworked, they will straighten up the exhaust mounting base by milling off metal. If this is done to only one cylinder, in one engine bank, the three cylinders' mounting base will not be in alignment. The only thing that can be done to bring the two exhaust flange areas in alignment is to add an extra exhaust gasket to the cylinder exhaust base that was milled off. The "E" series engine exhaust gaskets are held in position by two mounting studs and nuts.

It is virtually impossible for exhaust flange gaskets to seal when exhaust flanges are bent or the cylinder base is not in alignment. Sometimes, two copper asbestos gaskets may help. There is a thick copper blowproof gasket on the market that helps. However, if the exhaust flange is bent, the thick gasket will still leak.

There is a surefire fix for the two-stud gasket problem. Make up a thin stainless steel bushing that will just slip inside the exhaust stack. The bushing should extend beyond the exhaust stack mounting flange 3/8-inch so that when the stack is in position, the bushing will extend inside the cylinder exhaust port. With this bushing in place, exhaust gas pressure is relieved at the gasket so they won't leak.

The IO-470 and IO-520 exhaust gaskets give very little trouble unless the cylinder has been modified.

INDUCTION AIR FILTERS

It is surprising how many well maintained Bonanzas are flying around with worn out induction air filters. This is an item that should be cleaned at least every 100 hours, more frequently if you fly in dusty conditions. Your mechanic should point out the worn condition of the induction air filter. Airplane induction air filters are expensive compared to your car's more complex filter, but they are cheap compared to worn engine parts caused by dirt ingestion.

The original Beech induction air filter was made of screen wire, covered with a flocked material lightly coated with oil. This filter could be washed in solvent and reused. The big problem with this filter is the flock material wears off leaving the open screen which only prevents big bugs from entering the engine.

At this time, you have three choices in selecting induction air filters. The original Beech wire-flock filter, a pleated paper filter offered by Beech and the Bracket filter which is a sponge-type filter. Beech dealers should no longer sell the flock filter, but they will try sometimes to sell one. Don't accept this filter. The Beech paper filter and the Bracket sponge filter have both had their problems. The Beech paper filter has been cracking in the fold area. They are sluffing off particles of paper, so they are not perfect. The Bracket filter has had some sluffing off, too, and has had AD's issued against it for various reasons. There is another important factor that builders of filters seldom talk about; how much drop in manifold pressure do they cause? Loss of manifold pressure is hard to detect at low altitude, but at high altitude, it makes a big difference. Turbocharged Bonanzas are especially sensitive to loss in manifold pressure at the high altitudes that they are supposed to reach. If you cannot get manifold pressure in your turbocharged Bonanza at altitude, fly your airplane on a test flight with the induction air filter removed. If you get full manifold pressure with the filter removed, replace the filter with the Beech paper filter. If you still cannot get maximum manifold pressure at high altitude, then you may have a manifold leak, the turbine may be "coked" or a waste gate may not be closing. That induction air filter check is easy to make, so do it first.

Which filter do you choose? I personally prefer the paper filter, since I know the amount of loss in manifold pressure is low and the filter can be washed and is reusable.

IO-520 CRANKCASE

The IO-520 series engines have been plagued with crankcase cracks. These cracks, in most cases, are not the result of stresses imposed on the crankcase, but rather the result of internal stress in the metal itself, when the metal was cast.

These built-in stress areas eventually relieve themselves by cracking. Once the crack appears, the internal stress is gone. Unless the crack is in an area of the crankcase that is heavily loaded, chances are the crack will not progress. Continental Motors has set limits on crack length. If the crack is small, it should be stop-drilled and the hole filled with epoxy. Of course, as with any crack, it should be watched frequently. There are a number of engines in service that have the "light" case. If a crankcase has accumulated, say, 1000 hours without cracking, chances are good that it never will. When you are faced with an engine overhaul and your engine has a light, crack-free crankcase, it is wise to keep it.

ALTERNATORS

Alternators on the IO-520 engine have been a source of trouble. The clutch drive system originally had too few spot welds, so many would fail. Once parts of the drive system break, they fall into the engine. It means an engine teardown. Part of the troubles in the alternator drive system stem from the fact that the drive gear on the crankshaft is free to move fore and aft. The gear on the alternator is fixed so any movement of the drive gear must be compensated by clearance between the teeth. Continental Motors opened up the clearance between the drive gears which stopped the galling that was prevalent. There have been cases on factory-overhauled engines where the alternator drive gears made excessive noise. Inspection revealed that the alternator drive gear on the crankshaft did not run true. To correct this deficiency, the engine must be torn down. Since this is a defect in workmanship, contact Continental Motors for a replacement engine. It is good practice to inspect alternator bearings at 400-hour intervals. It is the inner bearing that goes bad, so I would recommend that the bearing be replaced.

OIL COOLER

The oil cooler on the Model 35 thru the G35 can be cleaned by soaking for a period of time in a good solvent. The Beech Factory would cut a hole in the tank side and scrub the inside tank with a brush, then weld the piece back. Sometimes one or several oil cooler tubes will spring a leak. Repair is simple, just weld the tube ends closed. As many as ten tubes can be sealed off without affecting cooling.

There are no thermostats to control cooling in the Model 35 thru the G35. In the Model 35 thru B35 a moveable door was added to control cooling in winter. In the C35 thru G35, winter cooling is controlled by placing tape over a portion of the cooler. There is a baffle inside the oil tank. Hot oil from the engine is pumped to one side of the baffle where it must flow through the cooler to reach the oil storage side of the tank. If this baffle cracks or breaks loose, the hot oil will flow to the storage side of the tank, bypassing the cooler. This results in high oil temperatures.

Since the oil tank is positioned higher than the engine, oil from the tank will gravity-flow into the engine. At one time, Beech had a check valve in the engine oil supply line but took it out in fear that it would stick and starve the engine for oil. The only means of preventing oil from flowing into the engine when the engine is shut down is a check valve in the engine. This check valve is just forward of the oil screen. Unfortunately, the check valve does not always hold, so if the oil level is checked on the first flight of the day, level may be down a quart or two. If oil level is down the first check of the day, run the engine a few minutes and then check the oil level. If the oil level is still down, add oil. If you add oil without first running the engine, you may cause the oil tank to bulge or even split. Excessive oil in the tank could damage the internal baffle which could cause oil cooling problems. The best practice is to check oil after each flight.

There is a way to stop oil from draining into the engine. Sometimes a too-long oil temp bulb is installed. This too-long oil temp bulb will hold the oil check valve open. Sometimes the check valve shaft will warp and bind, causing the valve to stick and leak.

The most common cause of leakage is a piece of carbon sticking on the valve face or seat. This situation can be improved or eliminated by removing the valve and grinding the face narrower. Let's say that the valve face is 1/8-inch wide; grind it until it is 1/16-inch wide. This will give less surface for carbon to interfere.

The oil pump, of course, is a very important part. This part should be overhauled at engine overhaul. It is a gear-type pump, and the gears can be replaced. Should the housing, in which the gears run, wear, it will open tolerance between the gear and housing, making the pump less effective. If oil temperature is a problem, the oil cooler is the first prime suspect, but in many cases, it is the engine sump pump that is at fault. There are two oil sump pumps available. Continental Service Bulletin 53-2 deals with the problem. The "E" series engine should use the high capacity sump pump.

The pump gear should have eight teeth and the impeller cavity should measure .940. If the sump pump is worn, or not of the high capacity type, it will not return the oil to the cooler fast enough. There have been cases where oil level in the oil tank would be low on shut-down, simply because the sump pump was not returning oil.

Oil capacity of the Model 35 thru the G35 is 10 quarts. Oil capacity for the H35 and J35 is 9 quarts. These were the first engines to use oil pans. The Model K35 thru the P35 used 10 quarts. The Model S35 and after used 12 quarts. It is really best on short flights to carry oil a quart low. As you climb out after take off, oil in the oil pan runs to the back of the oil pan. If oil quantity is carried too high, the oil level builds up high enough for the crankshaft throws to dip into the oil causing the oil to foam. This throws excessive oil on the cylinder walls causing the engine to burn and throw out about a quart. This means that the extra quart really doesn't do much good.

HIGH OIL CONSUMPTION

High oil consumption in aircraft engines has been a serious and costly problem for years. There are a number of reasons why they use oil. Aircraft engine cylinders use steel barrels and aluminum heads that are shrunk-fit to provide a tight fit. Sometimes oil will seep out of the joint where the head and barrel meet. This gap between the head and barrel will fill with carbon and seal itself. If it was my cylinder, I would insist on a replacement cylinder because, in most cases, the leak only gets worse.

The top portion of the cylinder runs hotter and expands more than the bottom portion, so the cylinder is bored on a taper. As the cylinder reaches normal operating temperature, the upper portion will expand to the point that the cylinder is straight.

Rings seat faster on steel cylinders which is an advantage. The disadvantage is that cylinders will rust especially in areas with high humidity. As the engine wears, the choke or taper wears out. The cylinders can be chromed by a special process so that the cylinder can be rebored and the taper reestablished. It is advantageous in some cases to have chromed cylinders because they do not rust, but it is hard to get rings to seat with chromed cylinders.

Continental Motors used chromed cylinders on their overhauled engines but stopped doing so. Now they fit new barrels to previously used heads, which is one big advantage to using factory overhauled engines. In 1981, Continental Motors started to use a different type oil ring which resulted in owner reports of 15 to 20 hours to a quart of oil.

Both Continental and Lycoming have had their share of valve troubles. Lycoming uses salt-cooled valves that are very expensive. Continental chose to use more exotic metals in their valves which resulted in the use of very hard valve guides. Valve guides basically run dry, so oftentimes wear. When tolerances open up, oil is drawn through the valve guides and the engine will burn oil. On E-185 series, Continental Motors issued Service Bulletin M-76-24TS, Revision-1, Supplement-1. This bulletin calls out a kit that seals off oil from entering the combustion chamber. If valve guide wear is excessive, it allows the valve head to seat at an angle and this can cause the head to break off.

On IO-520 series engines, careful inspection will sometimes reveal oil seeping from the hose that connects the various sections of the induction pipes. This means that oil is working through valve guides, so further checks are in order.

Oil in the induction system usually occurs during low power operation, such as taxi time. Oil in the induction system does not necessarily mean that valve guides are worn excessively, but it is a warning of trouble to come, so check for the degree of wear.

VACUUM PUMPS

You are getting oil all over the belly and your engine is equipped with a wet-type vacuum pump. The source of the belly oil seems to come from the engine crankcase breather tube.

Some of this oil is coming from the engine crankcase. How much depends on how good the piston rings seal. If your engine is of the IO-470 or IO-520 series, it depends on how high you carry the oil in the crankcase.

Wet-type vacuum pumps must be internally lubricated, so oil from the engine accessory section is allowed to enter the pump through the pump's oil seal. The oil, used to lubricate the pump, mixes with air within the pump and is discharged by the pump into an oil/air separator where the heavy oil falls to the bottom of the separator. The remaining air from the oil/air mixture is discharged into the engine crankcase breather tube which exits below the left cowl flap opening. As the vacuum pump seal wears, it allows a higher volume of oil to enter the pump, so the balance of oil-to-air ratio is upset.

The standard Beech oil separator is rather small but adequate to handle the oil/air mixture from the pump, provided that the pump seal is metering oil to the pump properly. When this imbalance of oil to air ratio occurs, the standard Beech oil separator cannot separate all of the excess oil. It is then discharged into the crankcase breather line and it winds up on the fuselage belly.

The right way to correct this excess oil condition is to install a new seal in the pump but this could prove to be a temporary fix. Fortunately, two high capacity oil/air separators are on the market that have more than enough capacity to separate the oil from the air. Basically only air is discharged from the pump so the airplane belly remains relatively clean. This is a good modification.

The Walker Engineering oil/air separator appears to be a better-built unit and has no AD's or bulletins issued against it. You can buy these oil/air separators from several vendors who advertise in the American Bonanza Society newsletter.

PRESSURE PUMPS

Dry air pressure pumps were developed which eliminates the need for oil/air separators. Some dry air pumps are vacuum pumps and work exactly like the wet pump except that they exhaust dry air into the aft engine compartment. The bulk of dry pumps in service, pump air to operate gyros. Air pressure developed by this pump provides a more positive gyro operation and at the same time gives improved gyro life. Unfortunately, dry pump service life is relatively short; 600 to 700 hours is about average. Vanes inside dry pumps are made of carbon so they run without lubricant. They run so hot that they sluff off minute bits of carbon. The original induction air filter for this pump was a styrofoam garter (Fig. 2-1). This filter would trap dirt up to a point, then the intake suction created by the pump would cause dirt accumulation in the filter to break loose and enter the pump. The abrasive dust attacks the dry carbon vanes which increases friction and generates heat. The combined load of heat and friction overloads the pump drive shaft, causing it to shear. Improvements have been made to the system that help to improve pump service life. An improved pump induction air filter (Fig. 2-2) is now available and in use. An air blast tube (Fig. 2-3) has been added to cool the pump. Downstream of the pump, a pressure relief valve is plumbed into the line. Further downstream a rather large filter (Fig. 2-4) is plumbed into the line between the pressure relief valve and the gyro instruments. On some Bonanzas, this filter is located below the instrument glare shield and just forward of the gyro instruments.

On the V35 series Bonanzas, this same filter is located aft of the aft engine bulkhead. This filter traps carbon and dirt particles from the pump. When it becomes plugged, it forms a dam in the system which not only lowers air pressure to the gyros, but causes the pump to work harder which in turn can lead to pump failure. Since this filter is considerably cheaper than pumps, it should be replaced every 200 to 300 hours.

The pressure relief valve is an often overlooked item. It, too, will collect dirt and carbon which causes it to bind and stick which in turn makes the pump work harder. For this reason, pressure relief valves should be cleaned at each annual inspection.

16

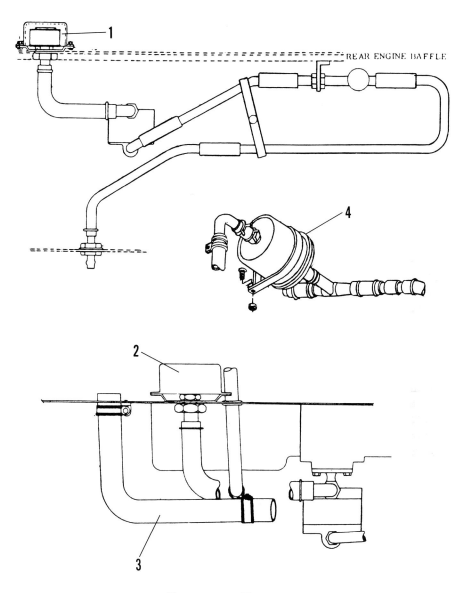

REAR ENGINE BAFFLE

**Pressure Pump
Figure 2**

When instrument air pressure drops, do not allow the mechanic to increase the pressure setting at the pressure relief valve. Do replace the in-line filter. If you have a dry air pump fail, replace the pump *and* the in-line filter. There are companies that can rebuild this pump at a fraction of the cost of a new pump. You may contact the American Bonanza Society for this information.

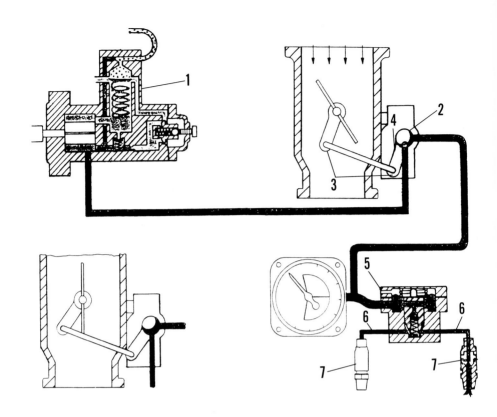

Fuel Injection System
Figure 3

CONTINENTAL MOTORS FUEL INJECTION

The Continental Motors fuel injection system is basically a carefully calibrated primer system. During normal operation, fuel is pumped to each cylinder in continuous stream. When the valves in the cylinder heads are closed, the stream of fuel continues to flow. However, due to the heat of the hot cylinder heads and valves, fuel vaporizes so that once the intake valve opens, fuel vapor enters the cylinder. The engine-driven fuel pump is the only moving part of the system (Fig. 3-1). Fuel pressure developed by the pump flows to a metering valve (Fig. 3-2). The fuel metering valve is a cam-shaped valve that allows metered amounts of fuel to flow through remaining parts of the system. The metering valve cam is ground in such a manner that at full open or full throttle position it allows an extra measure of fuel to flow. This extra volume of fuel is used to help cool the valves during take off or high power conditions. So it's important to use full throttle for take off and high power climb conditions.

The metering valve is moved indirectly by the throttle (Fig. 3-3). By this we mean that the throttle control is connected to the throttle arm that moves the throttle butterfly in the induction manifold. A second arm pinned to the throttle shaft links the throttle metering valve arm (Fig. 3-4). Through this linkage arrangement, the throttle butterfly and metering valve move in unison.

As fuel flows through the metering valve, it flows to a second cam-shaped valve located in the same valve body. This second valve is controlled separately by the mixture control so it can lean mixture required at altitude. It also meters fuel flow. After fuel passes through the metering valves, it flows to a manifold valve (Fig. 3-5) that is located on the center top side of the crankcase. This is the distribution point of fuel to the cylinders. The manifold valve contains a spring-loaded valve that shuts off fuel flow to the cylinders once the mixture control is positioned to the idle cut-off position. Six stainless steel fuel delivery lines (Fig. 3-6) attach to six ports in the manifold valve. These individual lines attach to the fuel delivery nozzles (Fig. 3-7) located in each cylinder head. Fuel delivery lines are all of the same length and their inside diameter is carefully calibrated to give the same fuel flow at a given fuel pressure.

Fuel nozzles screw into the cylinders so that fuel is delivered directly above the intake valve. Fuel nozzles are also calibrated and are lettered so that each nozzle will deliver the same amount of fuel at a given fuel pressure.

TROUBLE SHOOTING THE FUEL DELIVERY COMPONENTS

ENGINE-DRIVEN FUEL PUMP

Two types of fuel pumps were used. The early pumps had only a low pressure adjustment. In some cases fuel pressure at full power was marginal, so on later pumps a high and low pressure adjustment was provided. Engine-driven fuel pumps are capable of pumping more fuel than the engine can use. This surplus fuel flows through a swirl chamber (Fig. 4-1) within the pump that separates the vapor from the fuel and pumps this surplus fuel and vapor (Fig. 4-2) back to one of the main fuel tanks. In the early series Bonanzas, fuel and vapor were returned to the left main tank. On the later models, it returns to the tank from which the fuel is drawn. The fuel pumps include a pressure relief valve (Fig. 4-3) that can, and sometimes does, give trouble.

It is essential that the engine-driven pump separate and return vapor to the main fuel tanks. If vapor accumulates within the pump, the gears will cavitate and will not pump fuel. There is a small orifice (Fig. 4-4) that discharges vapor. Overhaul shops have overlooked this important orifice. If this orifice is plugged or partially plugged, the

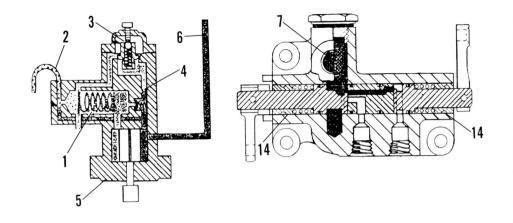

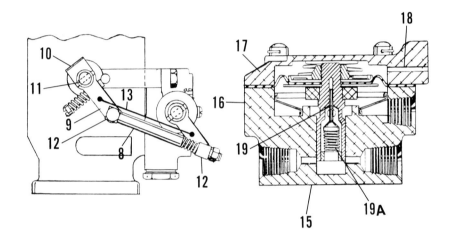

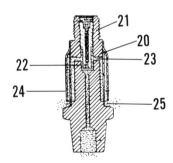

Fuel Injection System
Figure 4

engine will run just long enough to get you airborne and then it will quit. The fact that the pump has just been overhauled misleads you in dismissing pump trouble, so don't overlook the vapor return.

TROUBLE SHOOTING THE SYSTEM

When fuel delivery problems develop, go to the basic source of the fuel delivery system, the fuel pump (Fig. 4-5). Remember what you read on the fuel pressure or fuel flow gage, is *metered* fuel pressure. What you need to know is unmetered fuel pressure. In order to get this reading, make up a special fuel line (Fig. 4-6) that runs from the engine-driven fuel pump to the fuel metering valve. Insert a tee in the line and hook in a length of hose connected to a pressure gage that will read at least 30 PSI. The hose can be long enough to extend outside the engine compartment or long enough to go through the storm window into the cockpit. Start the engine and read the fuel pressure on the auxiliary gage. Idle the engine, at 550 to 600 RPM. Fuel pressure should be 9 to 11 PSI. At full static RPM, it should read 27 to 30 PSI. These pressures vary slightly with different engines, so refer to the Continental manuals. If you have to correct the readings by adjusting the pressure adjusting valve, then 30 days later pressure is off again, replace the pump.

TROUBLE SHOOTING THE THROTTLE AND METERING VALVE SYSTEM

The metering valve rarely gives trouble. There is a small in-line fuel filter (Fig. 4-7) located in the valve body. It is behind a hex nut that screws into this body. Clean this filter 5 hours after installing a new fuel tank and again at 25 hours after a new tank. Then every 100 hours. This filter is small and will plug quickly. The metering valve and throttle valve must work in unison (Fig. 4-8). The throttle valve is actuated by a throttle arm (Fig. 4-10). The shaft (Fig. 4-9) contains two arms. A short arm is connected by linkage to the metering arm. This arm is pinned to the shaft. The side face of the metering arm is splined and mates to splines on the inside face of the throttle arm. The splines are rather shallow and fine and are held together by presssure from a single castilated nut on the throttle shaft (Fig. 4-11).

If the splines are not properly mated during assembly or if nut torque is not sufficient, the splines will shift allowing the throttle arm to move independently of the fuel metering arm. This will upset fuel mixture and can cause the engine to quit. This looseness can be detected by opening the throttle half open and then by rocking the throttle control in and out by hand. Observe the throttle and metering arm on the throttle shaft—they should move in unison.

Wear in the throttle metering arm linkage (Fig. 4-12) can upset fuel mixture, especially in the idle mixture range. A good example—you land and advance the throttle to taxi and the engine quits. What has happened? The throttle has moved but due to play in the linkage, the metering valve did not move, so idle mixture was upset and the engine quit.

When linkage wear occurs, it is best to replace both metering arms, because the holes will be elongated and the linkage pins will be worn. Continental Motors has a spring (Fig. 4-13), Part No.628-371, that ties the two metering arms together to stop wear. Installation requires drilling a small hole in one arm.

On rare occasions the "O" ring seal (Fig. 4-14) around the metering valve shaft may leak. Since the metering valve contains pressurized fuel, fuel can squirt out into the engine compartment and onto the exhaust. The metering valve can be rebuilt by installing a new "O" ring which is cheaper than buying a rebuilt unit.

FUEL MANIFOLD VALVE

The manifold valve (Fig. 4-15) is sealed by the factory to indicate that it should not be worked on. The valve serves a dual purpose: to close off fuel to the cylinders when mixture is in the idle cut-off position, and it is the distribution point for the fuel lines to the cylinder. The valve body is made in two parts: the main body (Fig. 4-16) and a cap (Fig. 4-17) that is held in place by a series of machine screws. Inside the valve and below the cap is a very fine 20-micron screen and below the screen there is a rubber diaphragm that is attached to a rather fine spring. The top side of the diaphragm chamber is vented to atmosphere (Fig. 4-18). The vent hole is in the cap. This hole should be positioned to the side or back, never forward.

TROUBLE SHOOTING THE MANIFOLD VALVE

Watch for fuel stains around the vent hole in the cap. Fuel stains tell you that there is a hole in the rubber diaphragm. The diaphragm should be replaced.

At engine shutdown, the engine diesels or won't quit. This tells you that the fuel shut-off valve (Fig. 4-19) in the manifold is not closing. If the engine won't start, the valve in the manifold valve is stuck closed.

FUEL DELIVERY LINES

As stated earlier, the six fuel delivery lines that eminate from the manifold valve are all the same length. The lines are stainless steel with brazed-on end fittings. On rare occasions, these lines have been known to break, but in all probability they would show a crack long before they broke in two. Had they been inspected, the total failure could have been avoided.

I suppose it is possible for one of these lines to plug up but I have never heard of one doing so.

There is a seventh line coming out of the manifold valve. This line runs to the fuel pressure gage. On some of the earlier installations this line came off the metering valve. We will talk more about this later.

FUEL FLOW CHANGE AFTER ENGINE CHANGE

When you changed engines the fuel flow instrument in the instrument panel wasn't changed so the difference indicated in fuel flow is somewhere in the engine. If the engine runs good, chances are that the engine-driven fuel pump pressure is set correctly. The most logical place to look for the fuel reading difference is the fuel manifold valve that sits on the top crankcase. This is the valve that distributes fuel to the various cylinders. The easiest but most expensive, way to correct the trouble is to replace the valve. This might not correct the trouble, so remove the top valve cap. It is held in place with a series of cap screws. Remove the rubber diaphragm. There is a spring (Fig. 4-19A) on the diaphragm shaft that controls diaphragm pressure to the pressure gage. A friction-loaded collar on the valve stem controls spring tension that controls fuel pressure reading. If fuel pressure at the gage reads high, move the collar up the shaft to lower the reading on the gage. Move the collar down to increase spring tension for the fuel flow gage to read higher. Move the collar only a few thousandths of an inch at a time.

FUEL NOZZLES

Fuel nozzles are calibrated and marked to deliver a given volume of fuel at a given fuel pressure. Nozzles are lettered like A, B, C. All "A" lettered nozzles will flow the same volume of fuel at a given pressure. All "B" lettered nozzles flow the same volume of fuel but the volume is different than nozzles lettered A or C.

Since the same fuel flow of all nozzles in a given engine is important, all nozzles in a given engine are of the same letter. Manifold valves are lettered and their lettering should be mated to nozzle letters.

The brass main nozzle body (Fig. 4-21) has a very small calibrated hole (Fig. 4-22) in the bottom end. This is the fuel delivery end. Farther up the nozzle body are several holes (Fig. 4-23) that are open to the fuel stream and to atmosphere.

A fairly coarse screen (Fig. 4-20) fits over the outside diameter, and a shroud (Fig. 4-24) that is considerably larger than the nozzle body, is swedged to the nozzle body. The result of the shroud size is a space between the shroud and screen that is open to atmosphere (Fig. 4-25).

As the engine is started, fuel flows through the nozzle, creating a certain degree of suction which draws air into the fuel stream through the vent holes in the side of the fuel nozzle body. This air entering the fuel, atomizes the fuel to help in atomization in the cylinder. This air flow into the fuel stream is effective only up to around 1700 RPM.

When you overprime or on hot days when fuel boils in the fuel delivery lines, fuel will escape through the vent holes in the nozzle body and will cause dirt and fuel stains to accumulate around the nozzle base and around the shroud. While the stains and dirt are unsightly, it does not mean that the nozzle is dirty.

TROUBLE SHOOTING NOZZLES

Fuel nozzles will occasionally plug up. This can be detected by a cylinder miss or rise in temperature if you have a six-probe EGT.

Fuel nozzles should be checked for flow every 100 hours or annual inspection. To check flow, remove one nozzle at a time from the cylinder. Connect the nozzle to the fuel delivery line and turn on the fuel boost pump. If fuel flows out of the nozzle in a straight stream, it is clean. If the stream turns to one side, it is dirty.

Catch the fuel in a small can; check all six nozzles in the same manner. If the nozzles appear dirty, soak them in solvent for a couple of hours and blow them dry with compressed air. Clean the nozzle orifice in the same way. Never use a wire or similar object to clean the nozzle orifice, just compressed air.

FUEL FILTER SYSTEM

The fuel-injected Bonanza has four filter screens in the fuel system. There is a rather coarse screen in the fuel inlet hose in the fuel tank. There is a very fine 20-micron screen in the main sump drain in the left-hand fuselage belly. There is a third screen of 20-micron size in the metering valve body and the fourth screen which has 20-micron mesh is in the manifold valve. There are additional filters on the market that attach to the fuel manifold valve and fuel lines to give further filtering. My personal opinion is, they are not needed since a 20-micron screen opening is smaller than the diameter of a human hair.

FUEL VAPOR

In hot weather fuel is inclined to vaporize in the lines. When it does, you may get erratic engine operation and a fluctuating fuel pressure gage. When this occurs at high power or in cruise, turn the fuel boost pump on momentarily. This will move out the vapor and smooth out the engine.

It is unwise to turn the boost pump to high boost since it will cause the engine to run extremely rich. If you are anything below full power, don't use high boost. Never use the boost pump during take off or landing.

FLUCTUATING FUEL PRESSURE

When fuel pressure fluctuates, either on your carburetor or fuel-injected engine, it is most likely caused by vapor somewhere in the fuel system. Sometimes vapor is trapped in the line that connects to the fuel pressure gage. The line can be bled by loosening the line "B" nut at the fuel pressure gage and by turning on the boost pump or by pumping the wobble pump. Catch the escaping fuel in a cloth. If bleeding the line temporarily corrects the problem but after a short while it reoccurs, drain the gasoline from the line and fill the line with hydraulic fluid. The hydraulic fluid will stay in the line and will not vaporize so will cause the gage to read steady.

There are other areas that can cause fluctuating fuel pressure. An erratic pressure relief valve in the engine-driven fuel pump will cause pressure to fluctuate. A partially restricted vapor return line or orifice in the engine driven fuel pump will affect fuel flow. A worn "O" ring seal in a wobble pump or electric boost pump can allow air to enter the fuel system.

If a fuel line has been modified where a larger diameter section of line has been installed, vapor will build in this larger line, so go back to the standard size line.

It is not uncommon for vapor to appear during climb-out on a hot day. This is especially true if you fly a Baron. The vapor can be cleared out by turning on low boost pump. Never turn the boost pump to high position on anything other than high power; it will enrich fuel mixture to the point the engine may quit.

FLUCTUATING FUEL PRESSURE ON A COOL DAY

On a cool day you are cruising at 10,000 feet and your EGT suddenly starts to climb. The engine roughens slightly and you get fluctuation in the fuel pressure gage. If you were building up ice in the induction system, you would lose power but mixture should tend to enrich, so you enrich the mixture and EGT reflects the change and cools down.

As a precaution, check the in-line filter in the metering valve body, then check the *unmetered* fuel pump pressure. If you find fuel pump pressure out of tolerance, adjust it back to tolerance. If it fluctuates, replace the pump because the pressure relief valve in the pump is acting up. If you re-adjust pump pressure, check it again in about 30 days. If it is out of tolerance again, replace the pump.

If the engine gradually leans without fuel pressure fluctuation, the fuel mixture control may be creeping closed. Loosen the nut on the back side of instrument panel and tighten the knurled nut on the front side to add more friction to the mixture control.

One more thing to check. Look at the vent hole in the manifold valve cap. If you see fuel stains around the hole, the diaphragm is ruptured and should be changed.

IDLE MIXTURE

Idle mixture setting affects fuel flow throughout the range. To check for correct mixture, have normal engine temperature. Idle engine at 550 to 600 RPM. Pull out on mixture control in a steady but not too rapid pull. As the engine quits, watch the tachometer hand. If mixture is correct, you will get 25 RPM increase. If there is no increase, mixture is too lean. If you get more, it is too rich. To correct, adjust the spring-loaded nut on the throttle metering arm linkage. Back off on the nut to lean, tighten to enrich. Once you adjust this nut, you will have to adjust the RPM screw which is in the same area.

ALTERNATE AIR DOORS

Since airplanes fly in an environment where ice can be encountered, a safety alternate air source is provided in the Bonanza. Should the engines' induction air filter become blocked off with ice, or from some other source, suction from the engine will automatically open a spring-loaded door in the engines' induction system, providing an alternate source of air. The ram air effect is lost when the alternate air opening is the sole supply of engine combustion air. The air is heated to some extent so there will be a slight loss of horsepower, but the engine will run.

The original alternate air door (Fig. 5-1) used on Serial D-1 thru D-1116 was different in design, more complex than the design that followed (Fig. 5-2). This design remained the same thru the G35.

Starting with the H35, a dual alternate air door was used. The alternate air door system (Fig. 5-2) included a manually operated alternate air door (Fig. 5-3) that could be closed to shut off ram air. This would cause the spring-loaded alternate air door to open. In a way this can be dangerous. When using alternate air, it should be full on or completely off. There is an area where only partial carburetor heat will build ice.

With all the alternate air systems used to this point, there is a very remote possibility that high humidity air would pass through the induction air filter and would form ice inside the induction pipe to the extent it would shut down all air to the engine. This same ice can form over the alternate air door to the point that the door could not open. In this situation, an emergency landing must be made.

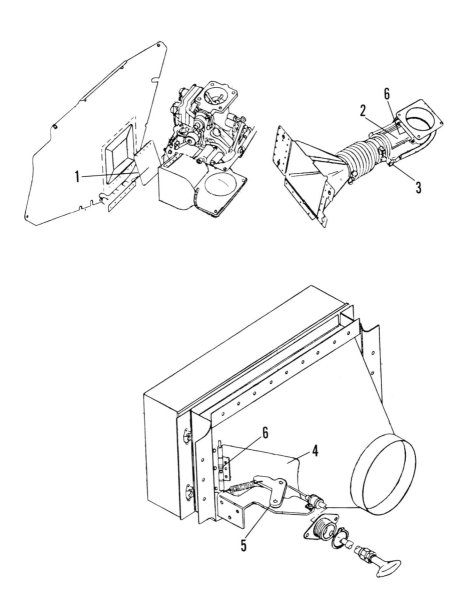

Alternate Air Doors
Figure 5

Starting with the Model S35 (Fig. 5-4), still another alternate air door design was introduced. This door has a spring-loaded arm (Fig. 5-5) that is activated by the alternate air control. When the control is pulled, the spring-loaded arm forces the alternate air door open. If the inside of the induction air pipe should coat with ice, the alternate air door will be forced open to allow heated air into the induction air system.

On all four models of alternate air doors, spring tension that holds the door closed can drop to the extent that at take-off power, engine suction will open the door to bring unfiltered air. This spring tension should be positive (Fig. 5-6). When alternate air door spring tension drops, the door will chatter causing the door hinge and hinge pin to wear to the point they will fail. This allows the alternate air door to be sucked into the induction manifold, choking off air to the engine.

HOT STARTS

Let's talk about hot starts on fuel-injected engines. If you read your owner's manual, it will tell you to start with mixture in idle cut-off position and to run the boost pump for a specified number of seconds. When you do this, fuel generated by the pump is being returned to the tank from which it is drawn. This may move some vapor but not the vapor where it counts.

When you shut your hot engine down and go into the terminal for a cool drink, heat from the hot cylinders rises and heats the stainless steel fuel delivery lines that are attached to the fuel nozzles. This heat is so great that it will cause the fuel in the lines to boil. This boiling fuel turns to vapor and can escape through the fuel nozzles. The nozzles are open to atmospheric air through holes in the nozzle body, and through the screen below the nozzle shroud. It is not uncommon to see fuel stains around the nozzle base.

By the time you return to start your engine, there is no fuel left in the fuel delivery lines. In order to get the engine started we need to fill the fuel delivery lines, but we must be careful not to flood the hot engine. So follow this procedure: with mixture full rich, turn the throttle vernier one turn open from the closed position. This will crack the fuel metering valve open to allow just a dribble of fuel to flow. Turn on the fuel boost pump and watch the fuel pressure gage. The gage will peak and oftentimes will fall back. Leave the boost pump on until the gage peaks a second time, then turn off the boost pump. If the gage reading does not fall off, leave the pump on only an instant and then turn it off. What we have done here is to replace the empty fuel delivery lines above the hot cylinders with fuel. Next, open the throttle 3/4 open and engage the starter. The engine will fire quickly, so be prepared to come back on the throttle. After the engine fires, it may be necessary to hit the boost pump momentarily to keep the engine running.

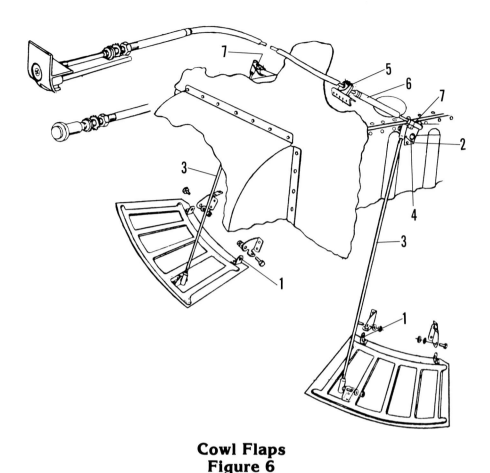

Cowl Flaps
Figure 6

COWL FLAPS

Cowl flaps always work. They may open or close hard, but they work. Sometimes they creep open or closed, mainly because they are not rigged properly. I see wear in the cowl flap hinge bushing (Fig. 6-1). They get so loose that they almost fall off. The cross shaft bushings (Fig. 6-2) get excessively loose. When this shaft rattles freely, it affects the nose gear door closing since the nose gear door actuator shaft turns on the cowl door cross shaft.

The cowl door hinge turns on a bushing that can be replaced. The cross shaft bushing (Fig. 6-2) must be riveted in place but it is not a big job. Cowl flap control linkage is often out of rig and most shops do not seem to know how to correct it. With the cowl door closed, the cowl door actuator rod (Fig. 6-3) should split the center of the cowl flap actuator cross shaft (Fig. 6-4). If the linkage is out of rig, loosen the bolts in the phenolic block (Fig. 6-5) and slide the control housing coming through the firewall (Fig. 6-6) in or out to position arm (Fig. 6-7) which will position the cowl door actuating rod (Fig. 6-3) until it splits the cross shaft hole. Once this adjustment is made, the actuating rod (Fig. 6-3) may have to be adjusted to insure proper cowl door position and clearance between the door and exhaust tail pipe. When the actuator rod splits the cross shaft hole as described, it forms a cam lock that prevents the doors from moving while in flight.

278 BEECH PROPELLER

The Beech Model 278 hydraulic propeller was first used on civilian airplanes starting with the Model H35 Bonanza. A similar propeller was used on the T-34 Mentor which is a military trainer. The two propellers look exactly alike; however, the T-34 propeller hub and the blades are thinner. So for this reason, parts from the military version and civilian models should not be interchanged.

In the H35 Bonanza, the engine crankshaft transfer bearing tolerances were so great that on a number of airplanes, governor oil pressure to the propeller was lowered due to excessive leakage in the bearing. This leakage caused the propeller to oscilate 100 to 150 RPM, mainly during climb out and cruise.

Beech came up with a fix by adding counterweights (Fig. 7-3) to the blades to aid in turning the blade pitch. Let's say the propeller required 700 PSI oil pressure to change blade pitch without the help of counterweights. With blade counterweights it requires only 500 PSI oil pressure. The transfer bearing would leak less oil at 500 PSI than at 700 PSI, so the propeller would run constant with the lower governor oil pressure when helped by blade counterweights.

In most, but not all cases, this faulty transfer bearing was changed at engine overhaul, where the correct engine transfer bearing was install-ed and the blade counterweights were *not* removed. This affects pitch change speed and adds weight. So they should be removed once the correct fitting transfer bearing is installed.

Most propeller shops set 278 prop blades too tight in the hub. This causes the blades to turn harder and requires higher governor oil pressure to operate the prop. When properly set, an appreciable amount of movement should be felt as the blade tip is moved fore and aft. It is a simple matter to set blade tension right. Just back off on the retaining nut (Fig. 7-2) one tooth.

Beech made a mistake by installing a zerk grease fitting in the prop hub. In the first place, the hub blade bearings required very little grease. Since the grease fittings are there, most mechanics pump lots of grease into the hub which winds up on your windshield.

Sometimes blade travel is restricted. Blade pitch travel results from

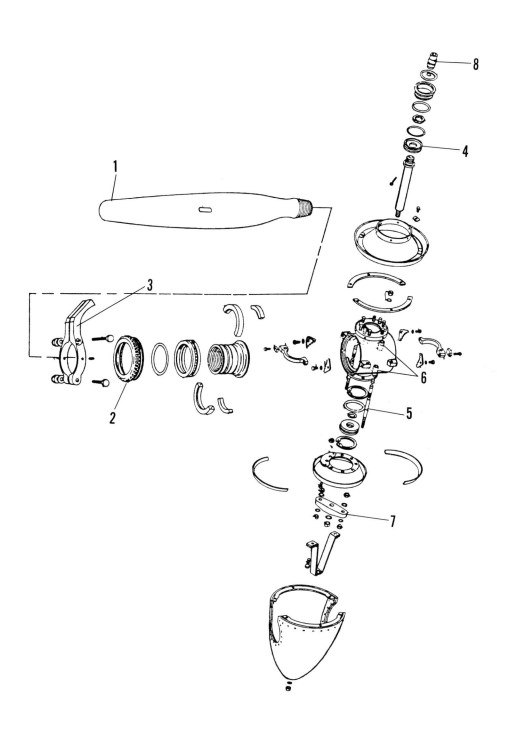

278 Beech Propeller
Figure 7

governor oil pressure being exerted on the back side of a piston (Fig. 7-4) as it works fore and aft inside the hub. The piston is sealed by an "O" ring that prevents oil from entering the front side of the piston. If oil does get by the piston "O" ring, it will cause a hydraulic lock and restrict blade travel. In high time Model 278 props, the cylinder in which the piston moves will wear barrel shape. This allows the piston "O" ring to leak oil to the front side of the piston which then results in the hydraulic lock mentioned earlier. The condition can be corrected by reboring the cylinder in the hub and installing an oversize piston. There have been a few AD's issued against this prop, mainly against the two pitch change bolts (Fig. 7-5).

The pitch change bolts move in two bushings (Fig. 7-6) that cause the metal in the bolts to gall. Galling is no reason to discard the bolts. Simply smooth out the galled portion and put it back in service. Part of the pitch change galling was caused by an aluminum yoke (Fig. 7-7) that attached to the pitch change piston shaft and to the pitch change bolts. Apparently this aluminum yoke would flex under load and cause the pitch change bolts to gall. A service bulletin was issued changing the yoke from aluminum to steel.

Some 278 propeller installations used an oil transfer tube (Fig. 7-8) which joined the crankshaft to the rear bulkhead in the prop hub. Some engine crankshafts won't adapt to this transfer tube. The prop works either way. The main advantage of the transfer tube is that it keeps high governor oil pressure away from the "O" ring that seals the prop crankshaft flange.

FUEL TANKS AND FUEL SYSTEMS

How long should a fuel tank last? This is a frequently asked question, one that is hard to answer. Through the years, Beech has used three vendors, Firestone, Uniroyal and Goodyear.

The Firestone fuel cells held only 20 gallons of fuel. They were thick walled and were heavy, but many are now 36 years old and have never leaked. The Goodyear tanks are thinner walled and are made of plastic material that becomes stiff and hard to handle when cold, so are shunned by service shops because they are hard to install. If the cells are warmed in an oven prior to installation, they are flexible and fairly easy to install. Because the Goodyear cell is a plastic material, fuel tank repair shops can't seem to repair the tank.

The Uniroyal tank is made of fabric and rubber, so is flexible, making it easy to install, and they can be repaired. In some cases, in both the Goodyear and Uniroyal tanks, workmanship is responsible for some leaks. Improper preparation of the tank liner inside the wing allows sharp edges of the tank liner material to cut the tank itself causing leaks. The lineboy is responsible for some leaks. When he jams the fuel nozzle into the tank bottom, he cuts the rubber. Improper tank in-

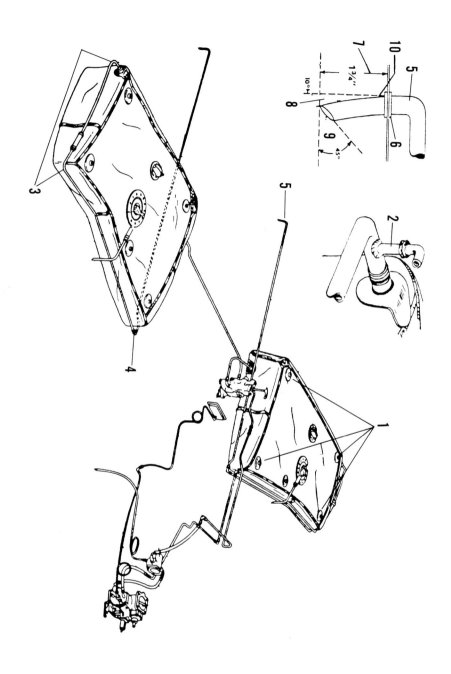

Fuel Systems
Figure 8

stallation, that leaves the tank bottom wrinkled with sharp bends at the top wrinkle, will crack the rubber. Tank sump drain nipples, vent and fuel return line nipples are made of special compounded rubber that is fragile and will crack and tear. You may have read that it is necessary to keep fuel in the fuel tank. The reason for this is that rubber contains plasticizer, a material that gives flexibility to the rubber. If the rubber fuel tank is allowed to stand empty for a period of time, the plasticizer hardens and will crack, causing the tank to leak. It is always a good idea to keep fuel tanks full. It cuts down on the volume of air in the tank and the condensation that results. Keeping the tank full of fuel will keep the plasticizer soft, but as little as a cup of fuel in the tank will do the same thing.

If the fuel tank was made by Goodyear, it is not necessary to keep fuel in the tank since it is plastic and the rule does not apply.

The Beech Factory uses two vendors mainly to insure a continuous parts supply. In the event one vendor should go on strike, there is always a vendor to supply parts. New airplanes may have one Goodyear and one Uniroyal, so it is hard to say what is in your wing.

Fuel cells are held in position by fasteners that attach the top of the fuel cell to the top of the fuel tank cavity in the wing (Fig. 8-1). In the Model 35 thru the E35 Series, there were snap fasteners that did a good job but were hard to fasten. With this snap fastener you might get all but one in position and while stretching the tank to fasten the last fastener, pull three loose. Bayonet-type fasteners replaced the snap type and velcro tape replaced the bayonet fastener.

The 20 and 25 gallon tanks had no baffles, mainly because of the size of the tank. But when tank capacity was increased to 40 gallons, the tank was so long that if a turn was made that would throw fuel to the outboard end of the tank, it would momentarily expose the fuel supply line in the inboard end of the tank. This would occur during fast turns, during take off with low fuel in the tank. This caused engine fuel starvation at take off.

Beech came up with a temporary fix by building an auxiliary tank filled with a net-like material that trapped something like a gallon of fuel. This tank could be rolled up and slipped into an unbaffled tank. The FAA issued an AD requiring placards restricting fast-turn take offs and restricted fluid levels in unbaffled tanks. As production permitted, baffles were added to the 40 gallon tank (Fig. 9-4). These baffles included flapper valves that allowed fuel to flow into the baffled end but prevented the trapped fuel from exiting the area. These flapper valves initially gave trouble but were soon fixed.

In recent years, specialty companies are building fuel tanks that are approved and seem to be doing a good job and, best of all, cost half as much. American Bonanza Society headquarters has a list of these vendors. The specialty people who build the 40 gallon fuel tanks build them with or without the end baffle. While the baffled tank costs more, it is worth it, as it gives automatic built-in protection from fuel starvation caused by fast-turn take offs.

Now, let's talk about the fuel systems in the various model Bonanzas. On the Model 35 thru the E35 (Fig. 8), two 20 gallon, 19½ gallon useable, tanks were used. There was an optional 10 or 20 gallon fuselage tank installation offered for these models. This optional fuselage tank was developed by Aircraftsmen, a Beech dealer in Oklahoma City. Their tank was 10 gallon. Beech developed the 20 gallon version. The fuel vent system from Serial D-1 thru D-833 (Fig. 8-2) differed from later models in that its vent protruded above the wing and faced forward into the airstream. On airplanes Serial D-833 and after, the fuel vent was changed to exit from the aft outboard end of the fuel tank (Fig. 8-3), flow forward, then inboard along the front edge of the tank. At the inboard front corner of the tank (Fig. 8-4), the vent line attaches to a 90° fitting where the line is routed aft (Fig. 8-5) and then extends through the wing skin. A rubber grommet protects the vent line from chafing on the wing skin (Fig. 8-6). The fuel vent line should extend below the wing skin 1-3/4 inches (Fig. 8-7), be bent forward 10° (Fig. 8-8) and be chamfered off at 45° (Fig. 8-9). Starting with the H35, a small #60 hole is drilled through the back wall of the fuel vent tube (Fig. 8-10) that acts as an emergency ice free vent. In the event that the fuel vent is bent aft, (mechanics working below the wing will do this inadvertently), the fuel vent tube should be repositioned forward. Always bend the vent tube *below* the ice free vent hole. If the tube bends in the hole, it will break off.

The reason the fuel vent extends 1-3/4 inches, is bent forward 10° and chamfered at 45°, is, that the vent line will be pressurized and will supply a like volume of air to replace the volume of fuel removed from the tank. If the fuel tank vent is bent aft, it will create a suction that will remove air from the tank. As fuel is removed, there is no air in the tank to replace the fuel, so the bottom of the fuel tank will lift and will continue to lift until all the fuel in the tank is gone. This lifting will not necessarily hurt the tank unless it chafes on a fuel level tab found in some 40 gallon tanks. The main problem is that the fuel transmitter floats will raise with the tank bottom, giving a full indication when the tank can, in fact, be empty and this will get your attention.

Now mud daubers love to plug fuel tank vent lines and manage to work the mud well up inside the vent tube. It is a good idea to occasionally run a wire up each vent tube. If it is plugged, it will be in the first three inches.

Figure 9-2 shows the location of an ice free vent. This vent is actually inside the wing and tees into the regular vent line. This vent started at the S35 and was added to some earlier models by the owners. This is relatively easy to install and is a good idea. Now, a 20 gallon fuel tank will hold slightly more than 20 gallons and a 25 gallon tank will hold more than 25 gallons and a 37 gallon tank will actually hold 41½

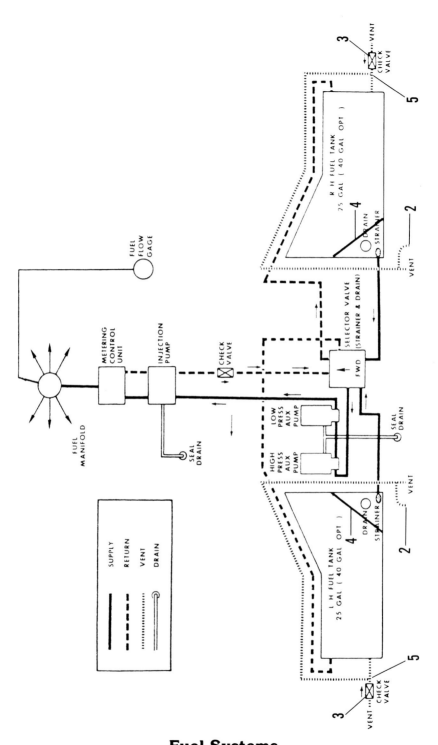

**Fuel Systems
Figure 9**

gallons. The reason fuel cells hold more fuel than the placard indicates is because each fuel tank has an expansion chamber. Usually, when your fuel tanks are filled, the fuel is relatively cool, but as the airplane sits out in the sun, the fuel picks up heat and its volume expands. How much heat the fuel absorbs depends on the color of the wing's leading edge. The darker the color, the warmer the fuel. If the airplane happens not to be level as the tanks are filled, it is possible to partially fill this expansion chamber. As fuel expands, it not only fills the expansion chamber, but it can also pressurize the fuel tank, forcing fuel out the fuel vent line. Once the fuel flows out the fuel vent line, it can and will empty a tank. Now, Beech engineers anticipated this, and built a siphon break valve into the system (Fig. 9-3).

If you were around when the fuel started to siphon, you could remove the fuel cap and the siphon action would stop. Unfortunately, we are not always around to remove the fuel cap, so the siphon break valve takes over. As fuel flows through the vent line, it flows past a line that is teed into the fuel vent line (Fig. 9-5). This line connects to a check valve that allows air to flow in one direction. The outboard end of the check valve is connected to a line that is open to outside air. This line is outboard of the end of the fuel tank and sometimes sticks out of the wing by one-fourth inch. On later models it is flush with the lower skin. As fuel flows through the vent line, it creates suction that opens the check valve, allowing air to enter the fuel in the vent line, stopping fuel flow. Mud daubers like to plug this vent hole and sometimes the flapper valve in the check valve will stick closed. In either case, you can lose a tank of fuel. Access to the siphon break valve is through an access plate located on the bottom side of the wing, just outboard of the end of the fuel cell.

The siphon break valve is easy to spot. It is red in color. The main body is 1-5/8 inches long and it is one inch in diameter. There is a hex nut on each end. To repair, unscrew the hex nut that has the word "hinge" embossed on the nut. Check the flapper valve for condition. In most cases, spray the hinge with WD-40 lubricant and reassemble the valve. By alternately blowing and sucking on either end, you can tell if the check valve is working. When installing the valve, note the arrow embossed on the valve body. The arrow should point inboard or toward the tank. Position the valve so the word "hinge" embossed on the nut is on the top side. This positions the hinge pin on top. Be sure the outboard line that is open to outside air is clear.

The fuel systems on the Model 35 thru the E35 were basically the same. They all used two 20 gallon main fuel tanks with the optional 10 or 20 gallon fuselage auxiliary tanks. Starting with the Model F35 thru the Model H35, the main fuel tanks remained 20 gallons but two 10 gallon auxiliary wing tanks in the wing box section were offered as optional equipment (Fig. 10-1). These tanks share a common vent line (Fig. 10-2). Each tank has its own siphon break system (Fig. 10-3).

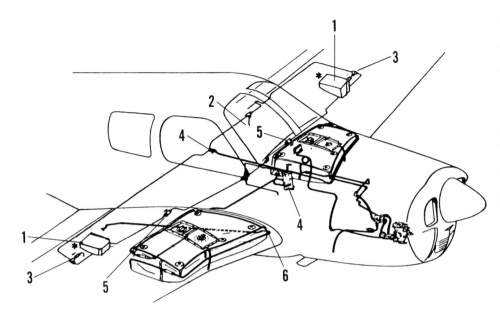

Fuel Systems
Figure 10

Fuel delivery from each tank is routed inboard into a common tee where it is routed forward to the fuel selector valve (Fig. 10-4). This means that when auxiliary fuel is selected, both tanks flow simultaneously. Now, in order to prevent fuel from flowing from one tank to the other, two check valves were installed in the fuel line, one in each wheel well (Fig. 10-5).

Sometimes, the two auxiliary tanks will not feed down evenly. One tank may feed down completely while the other tank may be half full. Once one of the tanks feeds down to empty, the engine-driven fuel pump will suck air through the empty tank, so the half-full tank cannot feed on down. The source of this trouble is the in-line check valve (Fig. 10-5).

Like siphon break valves (and they look alike), the check valves are spring loaded. In this case, the check valve that is giving trouble is in the line from the tank that did not feed down. It might not correct the problem if you replaced this valve, since the replacement valve spring tension might be stronger than the valve from the tank that fed to empty. The best thing to do is to remove the check valve from the line that did not feed down, disassemble the valve and clean and lubricate the valve spring and hinge pin with WD-40, and reinstall the valve. Be sure the embossed arrow on the valve body points inboard and the word "hinge" on the nut is on top.

Chances are, cleaning the valve hinge and spring will correct the trouble; however, should it not correct the problem, remove both valves, check them on a monomitor and adjust the spring tension until both valves open at the same water pressure.

The standard fuel capacity of the K35 thru M35 was two 25 gallon main tanks with 49 gallon useable and two 10 gallon auxiliary tanks. Starting with the N35, standard fuel tanks were the same as the Model K35. However, for the first time, two 40 gallon main tanks were offered as optional tanks. Most pilots want to carry as much fuel as the airplane can lift off the ground, so most airplanes were delivered with the larger tanks. There were a few exceptions, so it is a surprise to occasionally see an N35 with the 25 gallon mains.

All engine-driven fuel pumps will pump more fuel than the engine is capable of using. This is something required by the FAA as a safety factor. The amount of fuel returned varies from three gallons an hour to around six gallons, depending on engine requirements. In airplane Models 35 thru the M35, this surplus fuel and vapor was returned to the left main tank so on these models all take off was made on the left main tanks. Starting with the Model N35 this extra fuel and vapor was returned to the tank from which fuel was drawn.

Airplanes equipped with auxiliary fuel tanks should **never** take off on auxiliary tanks. This is a **no-no.**

Figure 9 shows the fuel delivery system of all Bonanzas after the Model N35. In the later Model 36 series extra fuel tanks were added to the wing leading edge but the basic systems remain.

Hand-operated fuel boost pumps were used from Serial D-1 thru Serial D-5330, H35. Three types of pumps were used. One was used from Serial D-1 thru D-1454 which was almost thru the Model 35 series. An improved version was used from Serial D-1455 thru D-2900 which was used into the start of the C35. The third and best pump was used from the Model C35 thru the H35.

Hand-operated boost pumps were the state of the art when they were installed and were great to build up fuel pressure for starting engines, but as a standby pump, they were hard to work and in case of engine-pump failure, would allow the pilot to reach a suitable field before his arm-weary body collapsed from fatigue. There are electric boost pump kits available on the market that would be a wise investment for your future safety. In selecting such a kit, be sure the motor and pump are in current production. Auxiliary boost pump pressures should be in the neighborhood of 14 PSI which is the maximum carburetor pressure.

On Bonanza Serial D-9948 (V35B) and after, the filler neck contains a visual measuring tab to permit partial filling of the tank. Filling the tank until the fuel touches the bottom of the tab indicates 27 gallons of useable fuel. Filling to the slot on the tab indicates 32 gallons of useable fuel. Of course, the airplane must be level to obtain these readings.

We have talked of fuel tanks lifting due to improperly positioned or blocked vent tubes. There is something else that will do the same thing. It is a leaking fuel cap. The fuel cap is positioned near the high point of lift on a wing. If the "O" rings that seal the cap do not seat properly, the suction created by the wing is great enough to offset the volume of air provided by the vent tube and the fuel tank bottom will lift. In most cases when the cap's "O" ring is worn, or tension is not sufficient, fuel will siphon from the cap. When this happens, the tank may not lift. When cap "O" rings show wear, they should be replaced with Part No. MS29513-232. If they look good, perhaps tension should be increased. This can be done in two ways, depending on the cap. In some caps, "O" ring tension can be increased by tightening a castilated nut on the bottom side of the cap. On other caps, "O" ring tension can be increased by adding shims below the cap's locking cam. Incidentally, the locking cam on the cap's top side will work easier if you add a drop of oil occasionally to the cam surface.

Water in the fuel can come from one of several sources. It can come from the supplier's tank, from condensation within the fuel tank or from water trapped in the cap's lock receptacle which leaks into the tank past the "O" ring that is out of sight. To replace the "O" ring, the cap must be disassembled. Fuel caps on the very early models look like thermos bottle caps. Just replace them, if worn.

Sometimes, if you find a fuel tank leaking badly and you are away from home base, it is always a temptation to drain the defective tank and fly home on the full tank. You cannot do this legally or safely. If something should happen to the full tank, there would be no alternate tank available.

There are times when we all would like to have more fuel capacity. In many cases, such as in the N35 Bonanza, standard fuel capacity was two 25 gallon tanks. There was an optional tank arrangement that was comprised of two 40 gallon tanks. Sometimes owners have asked, could they add additional fuel tanks to the wing leading edge, as Beech has done in some of their long-range models? Well, yes, it could be done, but frankly, the cost and trouble would not be worth it. The wing leading edge would have to be removed and the ribs replaced. A metal liner and new fuel cells would have to be added. The fuel vent system would have to be altered and then the hard part, FAA approval. We have talked of baggage compartment tanks available in the Model 35 thru the E35. There were two sizes, 10 and 20 gallon.

There are distinct disadvantages to these tanks. First, it puts fuel in the cabin and worst of all, it puts weight far aft, but it does add range. The easiest way to add fuel is by installing tip tanks. Tip tanks stabilize directional stability and do not detract from airspeed. They are approved to give an increase in gross weight. It is rumored tip tanks cause vibration. This is not necessarily true. There are a very few Bonanzas in service that have a slight amount of vibration which is sometimes caused by a frequency set up by a three-blade propeller. If tip tanks are installed on an airplane that already vibrates, the weight of the tip tank and its fuel will stiffen the wing and will tend to worsen the vibration. When tip tanks are installed on an already smooth-running airframe, they will not cause vibration.

On rare occasions, you may smell fuel fumes in the cabin. Check the most likely spots, such as the fuel pressure line to the fuel pressure gage and the fuel selector valve. Check for fuel stains along the wing root. If all of the above points are good, it is possible that the fitting (Fig. 10-6) is leaking fuel. This fitting is inside the air duct that brings in fresh air from the fresh air inlet (screen) in the wing leading edge root area. If this fitting is leaking, the only fix is to remove the wing to gain access to the leaking fitting.

FUEL TRANSMITTERS

The fuel gaging system on the Bonanza gives a rather accurate indication of fuel levels. It should not be relied on entirely, since the most reliable system is to figure time and average fuel consumption.

The 20 and 25 gallon tanks and the 10 gallon auxiliary wing tanks use one transmitter per tank to indicate fuel level. In the long 40 gallon leading edge tanks, two transmitters were used. The outboard transmitter indicated fuel level in the top half of the tank, and the bottom transmitter, the bottom half of the tank. Beech used AC transmitters that were standard for the industry until AC decided to no longer build transmitters for the Bonanza and Baron. Beech offers Kit No. 55-9018-1 which will convert the AC fuel transmitter and gage system to the Rochester replacement system. This change calls for some wiring changes. **Here is how it goes:** Post #1 on transmitter connects to Post #1 (cad) on gage Post #2. Center transmitter to post #2 brass on instrument. Post #3 on transmitter to Post #4 single outboard transmitter with case to ground.

The V35 fuel gage circuit is controlled by a printed circuit board for each side. If the gage is erratic, chances are the trouble is in the printed circuit board. Refer to Beech Service Instruction 1196 which deals with Kit No. 55-302303S. If one fuel gage is acting up, switch sides with the printed circuit board. If the trouble switches with the board, then it is the PC board. Over-torquing the PC board mounting screws can cause trouble, so don't over-torque the mounting screws. By the way, the PC boards are located on the back side of the instrument panel just above the fuel gages.

Those of you that must use a screwdriver to open the main sump drain door in the fuselage, might want to install a winged dzus fastener that can be turned by hand. Order 98-FM-2-5 stud, 31-804-100 pin and 98-2-MS spring.

In the J35, erratic fuel transmitter trouble has been traced to the resistance in the circuit breaker.

HEAT AND VENT SYSTEM

The Bonanza heat and vent system has earned mixed reviews. In the earlier models equipped with the "E" series engines, many pilots and their passengers complain of lack of heat in winter flying and lack of cool air in summer. Starting with the H35 the heater system was improved. There are fewer complaints on being cold, but there are still complaints on lack of air on warm summer days.

Here is a brief outline on how the heater works. On the Model 35 thru the G35 (Fig. 11-A), fresh air is ducted from the left nose bug (Fig. 11A-1) to an air mix box located on the lower left front side of the firewall (Fig. 11A-2). From there, the air is ducted across and through the firewall (Fig. 11A-3) to air ducts below the cabin floorboards (Fig. 11A-4) and to windshield defroster ducts (Fig. 11A-5). Air for the heater is taken from the fresh air duct (Fig. 11A-6), where it circles inside the heater shell passing through a number of heat transfer knobs to transfer exhaust heat to the air inside the heater. This heated air flows to the air mixing chamber on the lower left firewall (Fig. 11A-7). There is a valve inside the air mix box (Fig. 11A-8) which allows the pilot to control the mixture of heated and cool air to produce the desired air temperature in the cabin.

It is not unusual to find the heater intake air duct to the heater (Fig. 11A-9) collapsed so air cannot flow through the heater. Sometimes it is good to partially restrict this incoming flow of air which allows the air passing through the heater to pick up more heat. In some cases, the valve inside the air mix box is allowed out of rig and will not completely close off the air, so you may get hot air in the cabin in summer and cool air in winter.

The metal air mix valve inside the air box has rubber baffling stapled to the metal valve. With time this rubber will tear and curl and will not seal. This upsets the designed efficiency of the box.

Starting with the M35, the heater (Fig. 11B) was enlarged and moved to the right-hand side of the engine compartment (Fig. 11B-1). Intake air ducting was changed (Fig. 11B-2) but the principle of moving air through the heater remained the same. The air mix box was made round (Fig. 11C) and was moved to the right-hand side of the lower firewall. The principle of the valve inside the air mix box remains the same and the rubber baffling on the valve (Fig. 11C-4) will still deteriorate and leak air.

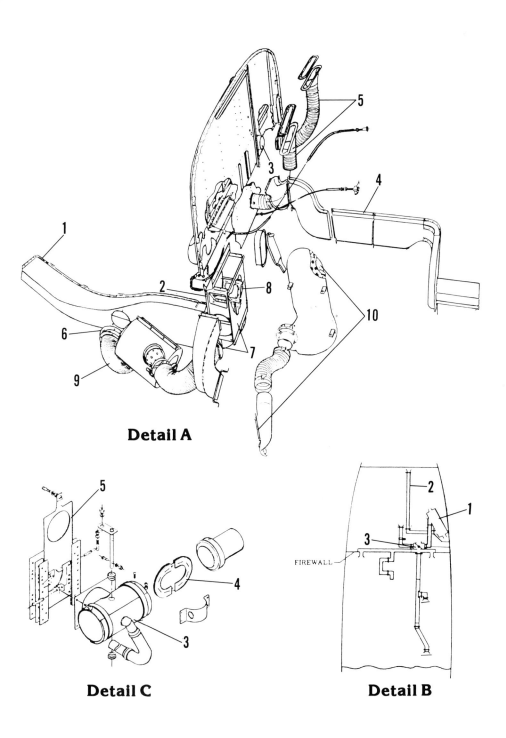

Detail A

Detail C

FIREWALL

Detail B

Heat & Vent System
Figure 11

43

Another important valve was added to this system (Fig. 11C-5). This valve is in the firewall. In case of an engine fire, it can be closed to shut off all air from the heater or engine compartment. Should heated air enter the cabin in summer, this firewall shutoff valve can be closed to stop all air flow. Of course, the proper way to stop hot air to the cabin in summer is to adjust or fix the seal on the air mix valve.

The exhaust heater serves a dual purpose. It acts as a muffler and through its heat transfer knobs, increases temperature of the heated air to the cabin. The efficiency of the heater is enhanced by flame cones built inside the heater. This is a cone-shaped device that quiets exhaust noise and at the same time directs hot exhaust gases against the heater shell. It is not uncommon to find these cones missing, so the heater efficiency is diminished.

The air ducting below the floorboards included bends and turns that are required to clear cross shafts and controls. The ducting is made of fiberglass and Royalite that can and does, on occasion, collapse. It is always a good idea to check these ducts for restrictions.

Fresh air is available to the cabin through the heater system and through fresh air vents (Fig. 11A-10) by the pilot's and in some cases the copilot's knees. Overhead air scoops provide fresh air to the cabin. In the V35 Series and the F33 Series Bonanzas, the fresh air scoops were moved to the aft fuselage, not because they were more efficient, but because they were more quiet.

The principle objection to the overhead air scoop was noise. The noise level from the overhead air scoops can be decreased by inserting a section of a bracket induction air filter in the air box directly below the air scoop. This is easy to do. Just open the scoop and remove the single bolt at the control. This will allow the scoop to be folded back to reveal the scupper or box to catch water. Check the condition of the sealer in the corners of the box. If the sealer is dry and cracked, remove and replace with GE silicone sealer. Cut the bracket air filter to fit snugly into the box. Check the water drain tube in the aft end of the box to see that it is clear, then reconnect the control.

There is another unwanted area that can bring cold air into the cabin. As the fuselage moves forward in flight, air enters the aft fuselage and flows forward until it reaches the aft cabin bulkhead. In many cases, small areas around stringers and controls are not sealed off, so this cold air flows forward between the fuselage and upholstery and exits into the cabin around the rear cabin window. It is this air that freezes passengers in the back seat.

The rear cabin bulkhead can be sealed from the back side by filling every small opening with sealer. If you have owned a car with an outside air vent, you may have noticed with the car window closed and an outside air vent open, very little air will come out the vents. But, if you should open the storm windows, air will suddenly flow through the vents.

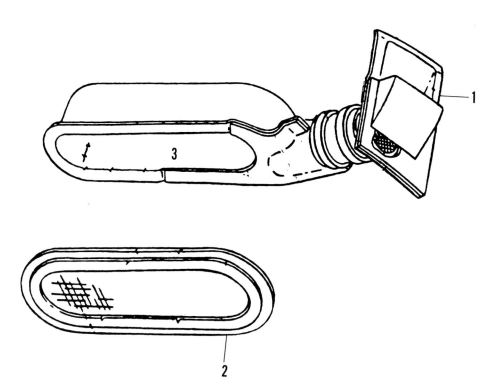

Vent System
Figure 12

In your Bonanza, air is being brought into the cabin until the cabin is actually pressurized. So Beech engineers built a storm window or exhaust vent system located in the fuselage belly directly below the baggage floorboards. Access to this vent was through a grill directly below the baggage door. This was a step in the right direction since it lowered air pressure in the cabin. However, in this location the vent was really not very effective. Starting with the V35, Beech moved this vent (Fig. 12-1) to the left side of the fuselage. It was connected to a grill (Fig. 12-2) in the rear closure bulkhead. The new vent system improved airflow in the cabin to the extent that cabin heat could be raised by 18° without any change to the heater.

Parts vendors quickly copied this new vent system selling it as a kit. This is a worthwhile modification, one that your back seat passengers will appreciate. The vent is also noisy, so if you can find a discarded bracket induction air filter, wedge the foam into the air duct (Fig. 12-3) back of rear cabin bulkhead. This will quiet the noise.

NOSE GEAR DOORS

During Service Clinic inspections, I have found the nose gear tire jammed in the partially opened landing gear nose doors. This is the way the system is supposed to work: as the landing gear is retracted, a cross tab pin (Fig. 13-1), located on the nose gear "A" brace lift leg, contacts the tab (Fig. 13-2) on the nose gear door cross shaft (Fig. 13-3). The upward movement of the nose gear lift leg causes the cross shaft to turn, causing actuating arms (Fig. 13-4) to lift. Since the nose gear door actuator rods (Fig. 13-5) are connected to these arms, the doors will close. A spring (Fig. 13-6) causes the cross shaft to turn under spring tension as the nose gear is extended and this in turn opens the doors. Now, if the spring (Fig. 13-6) breaks, the cross shaft may not turn. Then the nose wheel tire may jam in the nose gear doors. Fortunately, the nose gear will extend but won't retract during retraction. However, it severely overloads the nose gear actuator rod end bearings, especially at the idler arm (Fig. 13-7). When the cross shaft spring (Fig. 13-6) breaks, the lift leg actuator pin (Fig. 13-1) may jam in the cross shaft tab (Fig. 13-2), bending the nose gear door cross shaft (Fig. 13-3) on which it turns. If both cross shafts are bent, they can be straightened with care.

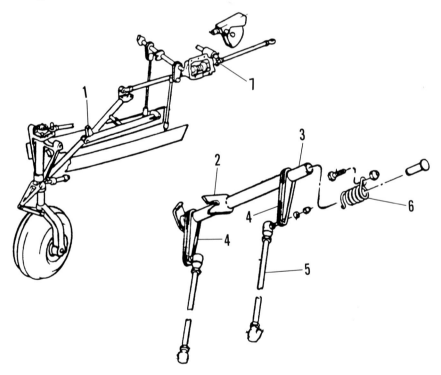

Nose Gear Doors
Figure 13

Since the cross shaft is seldom looked at, it is a good idea at each 100-hour inspection to reach up in the nose gear wheel well and twist or rotate the nose gear actuator shaft (Fig. 13-3). You could detect any binding or a broken spring (Fig. 13-6). If the nose gear door actuator rod is bent, the cowl flap cross shaft will also be bent. It should be removed from the keel structure.

To remove, remove the right-hand cowl flap actuator arm from the cross shaft and slip the cross shaft from the left side keel.

RETRACTABLE STEP

The retractable step used on all models of the Bonanza thru the G35 was really an ingenious device. A cable connects to the nose strut by a clevis and shear linkage (Fig. 14A-1). It pulls the step to the extended position when the landing gear is extended. As the landing gear retracts, rubber shock cords (Fig. 14A-2) or a kit made up of springs, retracts the step into the fuselage. During retraction, the step moves through two phenolic guide blocks (Fig. 14A-3) that form a track for the step. The step guide blocks are mounted near the rear baggage compartment bulkhead. When baggage is carelessly loaded into the baggage compartment, it bends the rear bulkhead, which in turn interferes with the travel of the step. This load restriction overloads the aluminum shear link (Fig. 14A-4) at the nose strut, causing it to shear, so the step will not extend as the landing gear extends. Sometimes, a wrong shear link is used. When the overloaded step cable tension is applied, the shear link does not shear but the step cable does (Fig. 14A-5). This step, when extended, can cost several miles an hour in airspeed, so it is worthwhile to keep it working. If the system is not abused, it is relatively trouble free.

FIXED STEP

Starting with the Model H35, the cabin was extended aft to the extent that there was no room for the retractable step. A fixed step (Fig. 14B-1) was used. The step support tube is mounted in a streamlined position, which does not induce the drag that was common to the extended retractable step. This fixed step is copper plated, then nickle plated and then chrome plated and buffed. In spite of all this protection it will rust. This step is so strong that in belly landings, the bottom of the step may grind off, but its support to the fuselage restricts further damage. Heavy passengers can overload this step which will cause the step support bulkhead (Fig. 14B-2) to crack. This can be detected by pressing down on the step and then looking for skin deflection in the fuselage belly directly below the step bulkhead. The step support bulkhead can be reinforced by adding a doubler to the cracked bulkhead.

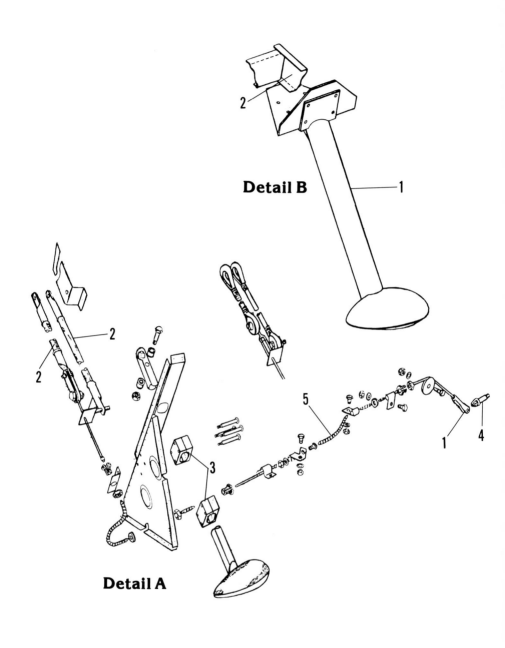

Detail B

Detail A

Step
Figure 14

LANDING GEAR RETRACT SYSTEM

The Bonanza landing gear retract system is positive. When the gears in the gearbox turn, the motion is transmitted to each landing gear strut by direct linkage. In the event a single landing gear fails to retract or to extend with the other two gears, some actuator rod or arm in the system is broken. There is a safety factor built into the nose gear retract system. Should a shear pin shear, the nose gear may not retract, but it will extend down safely.

Landing gear position light switches on Bonanzas prior to the V35B and F33 Series were activated by the arms on the landing gear gearbox. All that the lights tell you is the arms on the gearbox have moved. It doesn't mean that landing gear has. These airplanes had mechanical nose gear indicators that did indicate the position of the nose gear.

Starting with the F33 and V35B, landing gear position switches were moved to each wheel well. This gives a positive landing gear position indication. The landing gear electrical system is equipped with what is called a squat switch. This switch is located on the right main landing gear. Starting in about 1970, a second squat switch was added to the left main gear strut. The purpose of these switches is to prevent inadvertent landing gear retraction when the landing gear position switch is accidentally moved to the retract position with the airplane on the ground. As long as the weight of the airplane is on the struts, the squat switch opens the landing gear retract electrical circuit.

The bulk of belly landings occur on roll-out after landing when the pilot actuates what he thinks is the flap retract switch, but actuates the landing gear switch instead. In this circumstance, the gear will not retract as long as the weight of the airplane holds the strut in a compressed position. However, if a gust of wind or a bump in the runway causes the airplane to lift three-quarters of an inch or more, the squat switch will complete the electrical circuit and the gear will retract. Oftentimes the pilot may realize he has moved the wrong switch and quickly moves it to the gear extend position. If the squat switch is in the closed position, the nose gear will fold before the pilot can move the position switch back to the extend position. Mechanics, as a rule, will pull the landing gear circuit breaker when working on your Bonanza. It is the safest thing to do.

LANDING GEAR ACTUATOR RODS

Main gear actuator rods attach to the spider actuator arms (Fig. 15-1) on the landing gear gearbox on one end and to an arm on the landing gear lift leg assembly (Fig. 15-2) in the wheel well on the other end. The actuator rod is made of steel tubing (Fig. 15-3) in the wheel well end and is welded to a stiffened cythe-shaped double steel plate

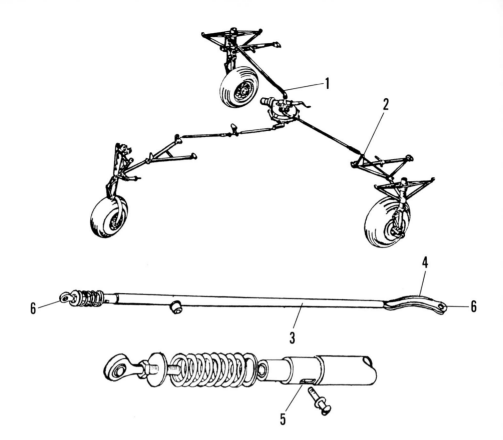

Landing Gear Actuating Rod
Figure 15

on the gearbox end (Fig. 15-4). The tubing end of the actuator rod includes a slip rod assembly (Fig. 15-5) that includes a collar and a heavy spring and shear pin that protects the system should something jam the landing gear in the wheel well. At both end attach points, self-aligning bearings (Fig. 15-6) are installed, which allow the actuator rod to twist as the landing gear retracts. With the airplane on jacks and the landing gear in about one-fourth retract position, the retract rod should rotate in both directions when rotated by hand.

The left-hand actuator rod rotation is slightly more than the right-hand rod, but they should both be free to rotate. If they don't, the rod itself will twist. The principal load on this rod is during gear retraction. This is a compression load. The rod assembly is actually longer than the distance between the gearbox arm attach point and the landing gear lift-leg attach point. The reason—when the landing gear reaches its down and locked position, this too-long actuator rod will compress by means of a slip joint spring arrangement (Fig. 15-5). It is the compressed spring pressure that holds the main gear in its down and locked position.

The actuator rod is in compression when the gear is down and locked. The slip joint is out of sight, so seldom, if ever, gets lubrication. If the slip joint freezes up in the extended position, and they do, it can cause the actuator rod to buckle in the compressed position. Sometimes the main gear actuator rod will get bent under compression loads. When it bends, it will bend in the sheet metal portion of the rod (Fig. 15-4) on the gearbox end. This bending results when the slip joint freezes but more often during take off, when the gear has just started to retract after initial take off, and the airplane settles back momentarily, to the runway. The gear may retract but will fold during the next landing. If the uplock block and arm should lock, landing gear motor power is great enough to pull the retract rod apart.

The nose gear retract rod is made in two parts. One section (Fig. 16-1) attaches to the lower actuator arm on the landing gear gearbox and attaches to an idler arm at the forward end (Fig. 16-2). A second rod (Fig. 16-3) extends forward from the idler arm and attaches to the nose strut lift leg (Fig. 16-4). The forward rod includes a slip joint and a spring (Fig. 16-5) that provide lift leg down tension. The forward slip joint includes a shear pin (Fig. 16-6) to protect the system should the nose strut jam in the wheel well. The slip joint (Fig. 16-7) is designed so that should the shear pin shear during gear retraction, the strut will fall to the extended position. The slip joint will not fall apart. When the landing gear is extended, the gear will lock safely in the down position. The shear pin looks like a standard clevis pin but it is not. The pin is made of a rather soft material, so always install a Beech-furnished shear pin in this location.

Both the front and rear actuator rods include rod end bearings (Fig. 16-8). The rear actuator rod end bearings are heavily loaded in tension as the nose gear is retracted. The Beech maintenance manual specifies both gear down and gear up tensions. Nose gear up tension is measured by attaching a scale at the nose gear axle and measuring the load that will just move the nose strut from its up stop. This load is rather critical for it imposes tension loads on the actuator rod end bearings, especially the rear rod bearing (Fig. 16-8A) that attaches to the idler arm (Fig. 16-2). In most cases, this rod end bearing will stretch before it breaks. It should be inspected at every 100 hours. Unfortunately, this rod end is covered up by a canvas boot (Fig. 16-9), so I would suspect that it is not looked at as it should be.

Rod end bearings look pretty much alike but that is where the similarity ends. Alloy and heat treat spell out the difference, so be sure the replacement rod end carries the correct part number. Bonanzas with 24-volt systems cause higher loads on rod ends due to faster retraction speeds.

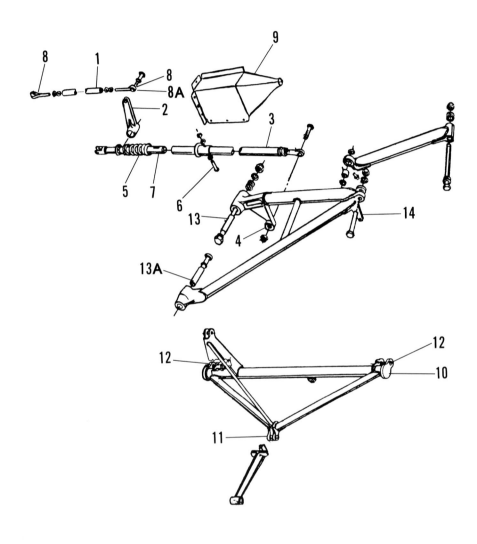

Landing Gear Actuating Rods
Figure 16

LANDING GEAR LIFT LEGS

Landing gear lift legs are made of steel tubing (Fig. 16-10) on the earlier series Bonanzas and a combination of steel and aluminum on the later models. Strengthwise both types are more than adequate.

Lift legs come in mated sets and are never sold individually. Since the knee joint (Fig. 16-11) is ground to break past center it calls for a factory jig fit. The main gear lift leg has two hinge points (Fig. 16-12) that are supported by the front and rear spars. End play at the lift leg hinge points is controlled by washer spacers. It is not uncommon to see considerable end play which is quite acceptable.

The strut hinge bolts will sometimes loosen and start working in the spar fittings, so keep these bolts tight to avoid replacement of these fittings. The right main gear front hinge bolt will loosen before the other hinge bolts, so check this bolt for tension and wear frequently.

The nose gear lift leg serves a dual purpose. It retracts and extends the nose gear and holds it in the down and locked position. It also acts as an actuator to open and close the gear doors. This part is sold as a complete unit since the knee joint is also ground to break past center in the extended position. The steel nose gear lift leg is heat treated so no welding is allowed, with one exception. Should the tab (Fig. 16-14) that moves the landing gear door actuator shaft, crack or break off, it can be rewelded by packing the surrounding area with wet asbestos. This isolates the welding heat. Starting with airplane Serial D-10084, the Model V35B, a new aluminum forging lift leg was used.

The lift leg hinge points (Fig. 16-13) are supported by fittings on either side of the nose gear wheel well keel. The nose gear actuator rod coming from the landing gear gearbox, attaches to an arm (Fig. 16-4) that is part of the nose gear lift leg assembly. This arm is located on the right-hand side of the lift leg assembly. The loads imposed by the actuator rod on the right lift leg arm will cause the right lift leg hinge bolt (Fig. 16-13A) to work loose in the right keel.

This looseness can be detected by placing the airplane on jacks and by partially retracting the landing gear. Push aft on the nose gear while watching the right-hand lift leg hinge bolt. If the bolt works in the hole in the keel, the bolt should be tightened. It takes two wrenches and be sure to snug the bolt tight. The left-hand lift leg hinge bolt will rarely loosen but the right-hand bolt should be checked at every annual.

LANDING GEAR GEARBOX & MOTOR

The landing gear gearbox in your Bonanza is a big mystery to a great many mechanics and to some shops. It is a means of extracting three thousand dollars or more from you. The gearbox consists of a splined

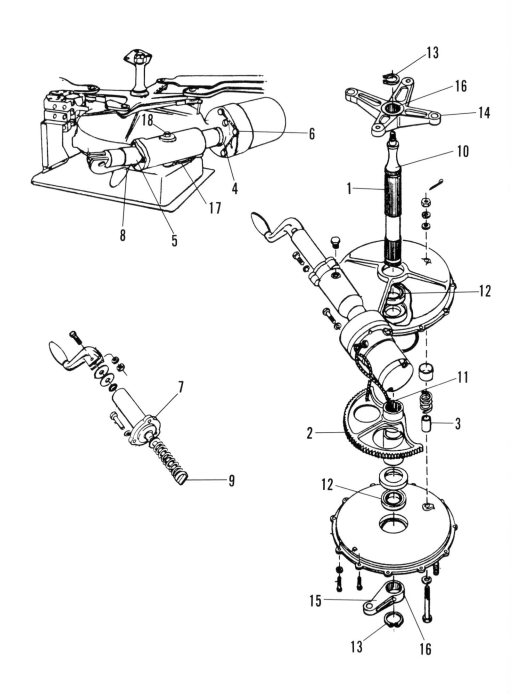

**Landing Gear Motor
Figure 17**

shaft that runs vertically through the box (Fig. 17-1). Inside the box, there is a brass sector gear (Fig. 17-2) that also is splined to slip over the vertical splined shaft. This brass gear is half round and is designed to strike internal stops inside the gearbox (Fig. 17-3). These stops prevent the sector gear from making a complete revolution should the landing gear limit switches fail to shut off power to the landing gear motor.

The sector gear is driven by a worm gear that extends outside the gearbox to accommodate the landing gear motor (Fig. 17-4) on one end and the emergency hand crank (Fig. 17-5) on the other.

The small landing gear motor drives the worm gear by means of reduction gears that operate within a gearbox (Fig. 17-6) which is part of the main gearbox casting. These gears run in hand-packed grease that is separate from the main gearbox lubricant. The emergency hand crank attaches to the gearbox casting with three machine screws (Fig. 17-7). This casting can be installed in one of two ways. It should slant upwards (Fig. 17-8). If it is installed wrong, the hand crank will not clear the floorboards. The hand crank end of the worm drive gear contains a screwdriver slot and the emergency hand crank end, a screwdriver blade (Fig. 17-9). This combination drives the worm gear when the emergency hand crank is rotated.

Should you retract the landing gear with the emergency hand crank, there is a possibility that an ear will break off the screwdriver slot in the worm gear shaft. It would then be impossible to extend the landing gear if the landing gear motor was inoperative.

In the early series Bonanzas, worm gear end play was controlled by a series of shims. Later-model gearboxes used a threaded worm gear and a hex nut to control worm gear end play. Controlling worm gear end play is important since the worm gear will shift fore and aft under load causing wear to the sector gear teeth. You can detect this end play by placing the airplane on jacks, breaking landing gear down tension, and pushing aft on the nose strut. If the main gear moves or bounces, there is play in the worm gear.

The gearbox spline shaft contains timing marks (Fig. 17-10) and so does the brass sector gear (Fig. 17-11). It is no big thing to time the sector gear to the shaft but it is important. This timing can only be done while the gearbox is apart. The spline shaft is sealed by a garlock seal at the gearbox (Fig. 17-12) and is secured in the gearbox by snap rings (Fig. 17-13). Remember snap rings must be installed with the sharp edge against pressure.

The landing gear gearbox is made of magnesium and is made in two halves. When assembling the two halves, seal the parting surface with General Electric silicone sealer. Two actuating arms are secured to either end of the splined shaft by snap rings. The actuating arm on the top side of the gearbox (Fig. 17-14) has four arms, two to actuate the landing gear and two to actuate the landing gear main gear inboard doors.

There is a single arm (Fig. 17-15) on the bottom side of the gearbox and this arm actuates the nose landing gear. On the Model 35 and possibly thru the A35, this arm was a magnesium casting. Needless to say, some magnesium arms broke, so Beech issued a service bulletin to replace them with an aluminum forging. This took care of the problem but, unfortunately, not all airplanes complied with the bulletin. Some of the magnesium arms are still in service, and are potential hazards. It is easy to identify the magnesium casting. It is fairly rough and is full of small pinholes, while the aluminum arm is smooth and has a small ridge running down its center. Both actuating arms have timing marks to match a timing mark on the spline shaft. We are finding wear between the splines in the landing gear actuator arms and the splines (Fig. 17-16) on the spline shaft. If wear becomes excessive, the splines can shear and this can render the main gear inoperative. Bonanzas and Barons that sustain serious nose gear damage should have the landing gear gearbox disassembled and the spline shaft checked for alignment. The spline shaft will twist sometimes just enough to throw one spline out of alignment. When this happens, it is impossible to obtain landing gear down tension.

The landing gear gearbox is secured to the airframe structure (Fig. 17-17) by a series of bolts. Sometimes these bolts will loosen which allows the gearbox to shift. This elongates the holes in the airframe. More important, it affects landing gear down tension. Proper lubricant in the gearbox is important. Beech specifies Mobil 636 grease be used. Grease fluid level should be only high enough for the worm gear to pick up lubricant. You can see this through the oil filler hole (Fig. 17-18). If the oil level is too high, it will leak out the emergency hand crank and all over the carpet. Unless the garlock seal leaks on the lower side of the gearbox, there will be no reason to add lubricant. There is a vent hole on the top side of the gearbox. If lubricant comes out this vent hole, lubricant level is too high. Use only recommended grease; don't mix lubricants. The Beech manual says that the gearbox should be rebuilt or replaced at 2000 hours. If wear occurs, it will be in the brass sector gear teeth.

I have inspected sector gear teeth with 5000 hour service and could still see mill marks. So if correct lubricant has been maintained and the gearbox has not been abused, there is certainly no need to replace the part. If landing gear motor dynamic brake is lost, it will allow the brass sector gear to contact the internal stops in the gearbox. This can damage the brass sector gear. In some cases the brass gear may bend which can cause the gear to bind and the teeth to wear. It also can cause the brass metal to work-harden until it becomes so brittle it shatters like glass. You can detect when dynamic brake is lost by checking for free rotation of the emergency hand crank with the airplane on jacks or in the air. With landing gear down and locked, pull the landing gear circuit breaker and rotate the emergency hand crank counterclockwise. It should turn 1/8 to 1/4 turn before the sector gear hits the internal stop. With the gear retracted, turn the handcrank clockwise and it should turn 1/8 to 1/4 turn before the sector gear hits the other stop.

The sector gear hitting internal stops is caused by one of two things. The gear limit switches are adjusted improperly, or the dynamic brake in the motor is lost. Motor dynamic brake is achieved by a two-limit switch arrangement. The actuator arm on the gearbox actuates a switch that cuts power to the landing gear motor. The motor is turning so fast that it will coast; however, once the initial limit switch cuts power to the motor, the coasting gearbox actuator arm contacts a second switch that feeds current to the unused coil in the landing gear motor. This will stop the motor almost instantly, provided the motor brushes are good and the motor commutator is in relatively clean and good condition. This check should be done at each 100-hour inspection or annual. Unfortunately, some shops don't make this check so you can lose dynamic brake and not know it.

On the Model 35, Serial D-1 thru D-2680 the B35, landing gear limit switches were located below the landing gear gearbox where they could become soaked with oil. Beech published a service bulletin and offered a kit that moved the limit switch to the top side of the landing gear gearbox. There are still airplanes flying with the limit switches in the belly and they give more trouble. It would be wise to move them topside.

How can you detect possible trouble in the gearbox? Look for oil leaks around the lower spline shaft. Look for oil leaks at the gearbox parting surface that would signal looseness. Look for looseness or working in the gearbox attach point. Look for looseness or wear in the actuator arm splines. Look for cracks in the actuator spider hub. Check for correct lubricant fluid level. With the airplane on jacks, cycle the landing gear and listen for unusual sounds. Landing gear and flap motors were originally surplus ammunition motors, used in World War II. Beech finally exhausted their supply and turned to a Wichita firm called Electro-Mech. The original motors were made by Lamb Electric. Both motors are almost identical though some motors seem to be better than others. The armature turns on sealed ball bearings.

Grease will sometimes leak out of the bearing, coating the commutator which insulates the motor brushes from the commutator, causing loss of dynamic brake. Sometimes a commutator segment will go dead. If the motor brush stops on this dead segment, the motor won't start and the landing gear may not extend or retract. In this case, pull the landing gear circuit breaker and rotate the emergency hand crank one-half turn and re-engage the circuit breaker. If the motor runs, you have an open commutator segment which calls for a rebuilt or new motor.

Generally speaking, landing gear retract time is 9 to 11 seconds. A 24-volt system was installed starting in the V35B Series Bonanzas. This is the same basic system used on Barons. The retract side coil in the landing gear motor is basically a 12-volt coil in a 24-volt system. This motor runs much faster than its 12-volt predecessor. The result is that the landing gear on these models will retract in 4 seconds. *No,* you cannot convert. The 12-volt and 24-volt motor brushes are the same size, so will interchange but the brush material is different. The 12-volt brush has a copper color while the 24-volt brush is jet black. If you use a 12-volt brush in a 24-volt motor, you will lose dynamic brake.

If it is evident that your landing gear gearbox needs to be rebuilt, I would suggest that you rebuild your own gearbox rather than buying a rebuilt box. If the sector teeth show wear, it is best to replace both the sector and worm gear. Gears, like bearings, establish wear patterns. Therefore, if you only replace one part, the other part will cause the replaced part to wear prematurely.

LANDING GEAR DOOR HANGS OPEN

Sometimes when you land you may find the right-hand inboard main gear door hanging open anywhere from one-half to one inch. The left-hand door may be slightly ajar or it may appear to be closed. We like to think that the Bonanza structure is symmetrical when in fact it is not quite. When the door hangs open after landing, it can be cranked closed by the emergency hand crank. What is really wrong, is the landing gear motor is low on power and the motor is telling you it needs attention.

SHIMMY DAMPNER

The Bonanza nose strut is not inclined to shimmy. Shimmy is usually induced by an out of round or out of balance nose wheel tire. New nose wheel tires may fool you. They may be out of round or they can be badly out of balance. The shimmy dampner does not give a lot of

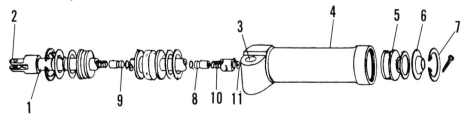

Shimmy Dampner
Figure 18

58

trouble, and some of the trouble it gives is caused by the mechanic who works on or around it. Far too often the shimmy dampner piston (Fig. 18-1) is found to be bent. This is usually the result of a line crew member using a strong tow bar hooked to a tow tug and turning at a too-sharp radius. Mechanics will over-torque the bolt in the piston, clevis end (Fig. 18-2), which prevents the piston from turning as the strut is turned. Over-torquing the shimmy dampner attach bolt (Fig. 18-3) will do the same thing. In both instances, this over-torqued bolt problem can be detected by jacking the airplane and turning the nose strut by hand. If the strut does not turn freely, decrease the torque on both bolts. If this does not allow the strut to turn freely, then the shimmy dampner piston is bent. I would say that the piston cannot be straightened and should be replaced.

SERVICING THE SHIMMY DAMPNER

To check the fluid level in the shimmy dampner reservoir, insert a 1/16-inch diameter wire in the cotter key end. If the wire inserts 3-3/16 inches, the reservoir is dry. If the reservoir is full, the wire will insert only 2-1/16 inch. To fill the dampner reservoir, secure the dampner with the clevis end down. Remove the cotter pin, washer and spring. Remove the internal snap ring and end seal from the barrel (Fig. 18-4) and fill the barrel with hydraulic fluid. Reinstall the end seal (Fig. 18-5), scraper ring (Fig. 18-6) and snap ring (Fig. 18-7). Be sure to position the snap ring with its sharp edge against pressure.

Now insert a 6/32-inch threaded rod into the floating piston (Fig. 18-8) inside the piston rod and remove the piston. Insert a second 6/32-inch threaded rod through the hole in the clevis end and screw the rod into the floating piston (Fig. 18-9). Pull the floating piston to the end of its travel, toward the clevis end, and secure in that position. Fill the rod with fluid. Reinstall the floating piston (Fig. 18-8), spring (Fig. 18-10) and washer (Fig. 18-11) and install the cotter pin. Remove the 6/32-inch rod from the clevis end. Reinstall the dampner on the strut, taking care not to over-torque the bolts.

NOSE GEAR STRUT

I have received calls from worried owners telling me the nose strut on their Bonanza has been bent. The fact of the matter is the strut doesn't sit perpendicular to the center line of the airplane. The axle does not extend 90^0 to piston center line, so if your nose strut looks bent, don't be too concerned. There have been numerous changes both in strength and ride control, all of which were dictated by increased weight of the airplane and improvements in manufacturing technology.

Nose struts from the Model 35 Serial D-1 thru the G35 Serial D-4865 were the same. A heavier and stronger strut was installed on the H35 Serial D-4866 thru the M35 Serial D-6561. A change was again made at the N35 Serial D-6562 thru the P35 Serial D-7309. Another change was made at the S35 Serial D-7310 thru the V35 Serial D-8598. The final change was started with the V35A Serial D-8599 and after. There is one thing in common with all of the various model struts. They will all fit any model Bonanza. Since the later model airplanes are heavier, it would not be advisable to install an early model strut on, say, an S35 or V35. It is good to install an S35 strut on a C35. Struts used on the N35 and after are larger in diameter, so if one of these stronger and larger diameter nose strut brace struts is installed on any model prior to the N35, the nose strut lift leg from the N35 or later must be installed.

No, you cannot just replace the single lift leg. You must replace the entire lift leg because the two parts that make up the assembly are matched sets. To replace, say, the upper portion of the lift leg on your own, is a risk because the lift leg must break past center the number of degrees set by factory tooling. If these specifications are not met, the lift leg can fold, which in turn would allow the landing gear to fold.

The nose strut piston and fork tubing (Fig. 19-1) were smaller in diameter on the Model 35 thru the G35. Like the later models, the piston and fork (Fig. 19-2) were shrunk fit to make a tight joint. By shrunk fit, it means the piston was submerged in liquid nitrogen and the fork placed in a moderately hot oven. Once the piston was inserted into the hot adaptor on the fork, the temperature of both parts would normalize and the joint was permanent from then on. As an added precaution, a bolt (Fig. 19-3) was inserted through both parts to insure added security. The strut axle (Fig. 19-1A) was fitted to the fork in the same shrink fit manner.

On all model nose struts that used a steel fork, the fork was heat treated so *no welding* is allowed. Areas to inspect on the steel piston and fork are at the piston and fork joint (Fig. 19-4) both in the fork and where the piston enters the fork. Inspect the axle for cracks at the point where it enters the fork (Fig. 19-4A).

The nose gear brace is a magnesium casting. Nose gear braces on the Model 35 thru the M35 (Fig. 19-5) used lightning holes in the front face of the casting. Starting with the N35, these lightning holes were eliminated (Fig. 19-5A). This later casting is stronger but its main advantage is that less water can enter the casting, materially prolonging the service life of the casting.

Nose gear struts are made up of the following basic parts: piston and axle assembly (Fig. 19-6), barrel (Fig. 19-7), rebound control (Fig. 19-8), nose gear brace (Fig. 19-9), and strut cap (Fig. 19-10).

The nose barrel is the part in which the piston assembly moves up and down. There are two brass bushings inside the barrel (Fig. 19-11).

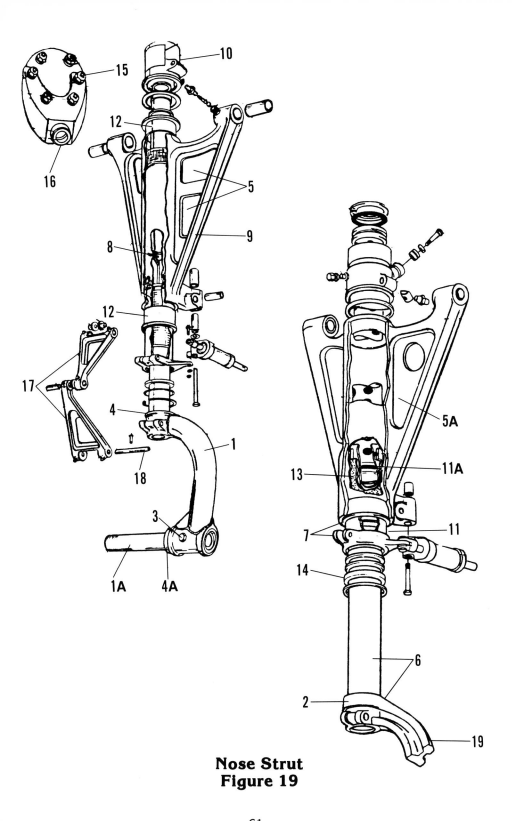

Nose Strut
Figure 19

One bearing is at the lower end of the barrel and it is this bearing that will show wear. The second bearing is located midway inside the barrel (Fig. 19-11A). This bearing is grooved to accept an "O" ring seal and it is this seal that holds oil and air in the strut. The magnesium nose gear brace has two brass bearings (Fig. 19-12), one at the top end and one at the bottom end. The strut barrel turns in the brace bearings which allows the airplane to be steered. Here again, the lower brace bearing will wear since it is exposed to dirt.

The bearings inside the barrel assembly are brazed in position by a resistance welding method. This method of welding minimizes warpage, but it makes repair difficult. Delta Engineering has learned to replace these bearings at reasonable cost.

Two felt pads are used inside the strut (Fig. 19-13). A thick felt pad soaked with SAE 30 oil is fitted inside the strut barrel and lays between the two bearings inside the barrel. The purpose of this felt pad is twofold. It lubricates the strut piston and it helps to keep dirt out of the barrel. The bottom end of the strut barrel is recessed and grooved to accommodate a scraper ring (Fig. 19-14). This scrapes dirt from the piston and snap rings that hold the scraper ring in place.

If you disassemble a nose strut, handle this scraper ring with extreme care. The lower edge of the scraper ring that contacts the chrome piston will hone to a razor edge and can easily cut your hand.

The felt pad inside the lower nose strut brace is also soaked in SAE 30 motor oil. This pad is exposed to water that enters through the lightning holes in the nose gear brace and through the lower bearing in the brace. The volume of water entering the brace can be reduced by covering the lightning holes with duct tape or some other protective covering.

Over a period of time, water will drive the lubricant from the felt pad inside the brace. This water remains in the felt pad and causes the magnesium to corrode. The result is that the lower strut brace will corrode to the point that it looks like a piece of old lace. This can ruin the brace; at the same time the corrosion prevents the strut barrel from turning, making it difficult to steer the airplane. This condition should be checked at every 100-hour inspection.

A rebound assembly is positioned inside the strut barrel (Fig. 19-8). This assembly serves a dual purpose. It dampens bounce and acts as a shock absorber. The second duty of the rebound control is to hold the strut together when in extended position. A strut cap tops the nose strut assembly and is held in position by a series of stud bolts (Fig. 19-15), positioned in the top of the strut barrel. These stud bolts are brazed in position in the barrel and will pull out if overtorqued. Endplay between the strut cap and brace assembly is controlled by a laminated shim. One-and-a-half to three-thousandths-inch clearance is desirable between the cap and brace. The strut cap includes an adapter that holds a sealed ball bearing (Fig. 19-16). This bearing picks up a track, riveted to the nose structure and straightens the strut during the retract cycle.

When the F-225-8 engine was first used in the G35, the rudder pedals would kick as the landing gear was in mid-retraction. This was caused by the increase in engine torque that required more rudder, which caused the nose strut to turn more during take off. This caused the straightener roller to pick up the straightener track sooner, which made the rudder pedals kick. In order to correct this condition, the straightener track had to be repositioned. Unfortunately, all tracks were not repositioned, so the rudder kick condition may still exist.

The torque knees (Fig. 19-17) connect the lower strut barrel and the piston and axle. The lower torque knee pin (Fig. 19-18) serves a dual purpose. It not only is used to connect the barrel and piston and axle assembly, but acts as an attach point for the tow bar. This pin is designed weak structurally, so that if too strong a tow bar is used and is turned beyond the strut travel stops, the pin will break and prevent damage to the strut. So you see, this pin is also a fuse of sorts.

Starting with Serial D-6562 the N35, a different rebound control was used inside the strut. This rebound control will no longer hold the strut together. The torque knees on these models now prevent the strut from coming apart when extended. The lower torque knee includes an anvil that contacts an anvil on the strut fork. With this strut retention system, never disconnect the torque knee scissor bolt while the strut is extended. If you do, the strut piston and axle and fluid will squirt violently out on the floor. Starting with Serial D-7252 the P35, the nose gear fork was changed from steel to an aluminum forging (Fig. 19-19). One of the felt pads inside the strut was eliminated and the rebound control was changed to give a different ride.

MUD SCRAPERS

You have to watch how nose wheel mud scrapers are installed. You see, at 80 miles per hour, the nose wheel tire grows a considerable amount in diameter. If the mud scraper is positioned too close to the tire, it will mill off rubber from the expanded tire. On the newer model airplane this mud scraper was omitted. If you don't fly off of grass fields I would remove the scraper.

MAIN GEAR SHOCK STRUTS

Let's go to the main gear shocks. The main landing gear shock absorbers rarely show wear in the barrel bearings, since unlike the nose gear, the bearings are isolated from dirt. The trunion or hinge bushings will sometimes show wear which is relatively easy to fix.

Like the nose strut, changes were made to strengthen the strut as airplane gross weight was increased.

Here is where the model changes were made:

Model 35	Serial D-1	thru	D-2680	B35
C35	D-2681	thru	D-4098	Mid F35
Mid F35	D-4099	thru	D-4865	G35
H35	D-4866	thru	D-7132	Mid P35
Latter P35	D-7133	and after.		

The primary design remained the same until Serial D-7133 the late P35, where a major change in material was made. Up to this change, the primary changes were increasing strut piston size, changes in rebound control and rod design. Starting with airplane Serial D-5791 and after, anvils were added to torque knees. It not only limited strut extension travel, but held the strut together when in the extended position. So don't remove the torque knee scissor bolt unless the air pressure inside the strut has been released.

Like the nose strut, the main gear barrel contains two brass bushings that position the piston assembly in the barrel. The lower bearing guides the piston while the second bearing, located about midpoint in the barrel is grooved to hold an "O" ring seal that seals oil and air inside the strut. The forging that holds the strut piston and axle (Fig. 20-1), the upper barrel, (Fig. 20-2) and the brace assembly are heat treated, so if cracked or damaged, they cannot be repaired. There is an "O" ring seal and plate that holds a Shrader air valve (Fig. 20-3) that seals the top end of the strut barrel. This plate is held in position by a snap ring. It is absolutely essential that the snap ring be positioned with its sharp edge against pressure. If the snap ring is installed improperly, pressure will work out of its groove and allow the top plate to blow a three-inch hole in the top wing skin, and this will ruin your day! If a hole is blown in the wing, and this has happened, install a flush patch on the wing skin to minimize the damage.

Starting with airplane Serial D-7133 and after (middle of the P35 Series), the main gear barrel and braces (Fig. 20-4) were changed to aluminum forging and aluminum extrusion. The barrel starts out as a solid aluminum forging which is X-rayed before any machine work is done. If free of flaws, the forging is bored out and attach fittings milled out (Fig. 20-5).

The lower barrel bushing threads into the barrel and the center bearing is grooved to take two "O" rings, one to seal the bearing to the barrel and the inner ring to seal the piston that holds air and fluid in the barrel. This bearing is held in position in the barrel by huck bolts. The inner "O" ring seal groove in the center barrel bearing is cut oversize to accommodate two nylon rings that prevent the "O" ring from twisting as the piston moves on the "O" ring. The aluminum forging side braces (Fig. 20-8) bolt or pin to the main support forging that in-

64

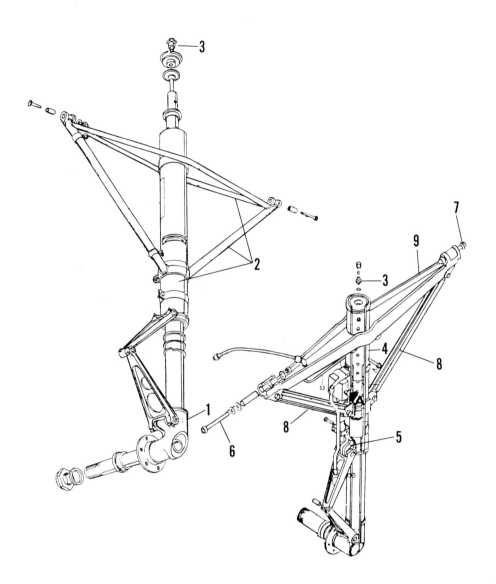

**Main Gear Shock Struts
Figure 20**

cludes the strut hinge support (Fig. 20-9). This strut is stronger and lighter in weight and it can be repaired in the field. Like its predecessor, the torque knees hold the strut together when in the extended position.

Strut pistons on all Bonanzas are initially ground slightly undersize, are copper plated, then chrome plated and ground to size. If the chrome wears thin, it can be stripped and replated.

Main gear struts can be changed from model to model but never install an earlier model strut on a later model Bonanza. Don't mix models on a given airplane since different rebound controls give different rides. Normally, nose gear extension is five inches, main gear is three inches. Remember, oil in the strut provides the quality of ride while air or nitrogen determines the strut extension. If a strut acts like a worn out shock absorber on a car, chances are it needs hydraulic oil.

It is essential that landing gear strut hinge bolt (Fig. 20-6-7) torque be maintained so the bolts will not move in the hinge bolt adapters in the wing spars of the main gear. The same applies to the nose keel in the case of the nose gear. A rule of thumb for checking shock strut bolt tension is, with the airplane on jacks, break landing gear down tension and lift the main gear by hand. Watch for hinge bolt deflection as you lift. Watch to see if the bolt turns as the strut is lifted. It is usually the front, right-hand main gear hinge bolt (Fig. 20-7) that will loosen. If the bolts have been working for some time, vew bushings may be required. As you lift the nose gear, watch the hinge bolts for rotating with the strut. Apply side pressure by rocking the strut sideways and look for hinge bolt looseness.

It is not uncommon to find wheel bearing tension loose. With the airplane on jacks, spin the nose wheel and listen as the bearing spins. You can detect a rough or dry bearing by listening. Watch the grease seal in the wheel as the wheel spins. The seal should not move in the wheel. If it spins, tighten the wheel bearing tension. Also grasp the wheel at the top and bottom position and rock the wheel. There should be no free play.

Any time you change tires, always run a gear retraction to see that the tires clear the wheel well. Just because the tire is new, doesn't mean it cannot be oversize. Spin the wheel and watch the tire to see if it is truly round. Lots of new tires are not round. If the tire is out of balance, it will shake the airframe on take off. If it is out of round, it won't balance, so take the tire back. The factory does.

LANDING GEAR MOTOR

Landing gear retract time varies from model to model, but on the 12-volt systems it runs from 15 seconds on the Model 35 and 8 to 11 seconds on the S35. In the Model 35 series, a relay was positioned close to the landing gear motor which insured a good current supply to the landing gear motor. This relay was omitted on later models. Wire size to the landing gear motor, while adequate, was marginal. The length of wire from the squat switch to the motor circuit built up line resistance to the point that should resistance in the circuit build, even in small amounts, electrical power to the landing gear motor would drop enough to slow the motor down.

Starting in the Model V35B series, a second landing gear squat switch was added. This was the straw that broke the camel's back. A relay was again added to the landing gear motor power supply. Beech Service Instruction 0943 Rev. 1 covers installation of a relay which is furnished in Beech Kit 35-2015-1 S.

If you notice a change in your landing gear retract time, have the landing gear electrical circuit checked for high resistance. The most logical point for high resistance is across the limit switch points. You see, dirt will work into the limit switch and the points will burn, causing high resistance. If any resistance or drop in current is noted, replace the micro-switch. Of course, high resistance can be found in any wire connection. The landing gear motor draws 35 amps when loaded, so it needs power. A motor needing repair will also slow gear retraction. When retract time slows down, the landing gear motor and electrical system are crying for attention.

THE LANDING GEAR UPLOCK BLOCK

The purpose of the uplock block and roller is to prevent the main landing gear from moving out of the wheel wells during pull ups or under turbulent conditions. Should the landing gear move under these conditions, it would cause the landing gear doors to open. This would allow air pressure to enter the wheel well, and could in turn cause structural damage.

Here is how the system works. As the main gear reaches its almost-up or retracted position, cable (Fig. 21-1) pulls block (Fig. 21-2) downward, positioning the block end directly in front of the roller (Fig. 21-3). The roller is attached to the main landing gear lift leg knee joint. When the landing gear is fully retracted, the block is directly in front of the roller. The block is adjusted to allow 10 to 20 thousandths inch clearance between the block and roller. The block is serrated so that it can be adjusted. There is a spring (Fig. 21-4) that pulls the block up out of position when the cable tension is relaxed. The uplock cable is connected to a bellcrank that, in turn, is connected to the inboard door actuator rod.

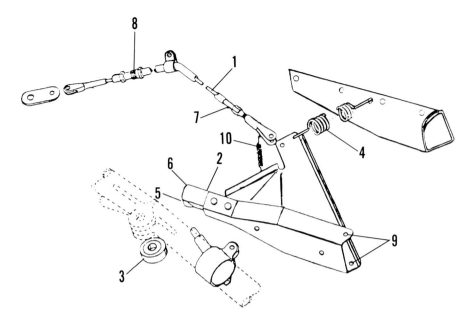

Landing Gear Uplock Block
Figure 21

If the system is adjusted properly, the block should never touch the roller, but it is not uncommon to find that it does. In fact, in some cases, the block may contact the roller on the block's lower radius (Fig. 21-5). This means that the block is making hard contact. It is easy to spot this condition by looking for polished marks on the end of the uplock block (Fig. 21-6).

Assuming that the uplock block roller clearance is 10 to 20 thousandths inch, the source of trouble is incorrect cable tension (Fig. 21-1). Correct cable tension is 52-1/2 lbs. If cable tension is too high, it pulls the block in position too soon. If the cable tension is low, it pulls the block in position late. In either case, the block is pulled in position out of time. The cable can be adjusted by a turnbuckle (Fig. 21-7) or by shifting the cable at the wing root rib (Fig. 21-8). The spring (Fig. 21-4) tends to rust badly and will stretch causing the block to contact the roller. The airplane should not be flown if this spring is broken. There is a good chance that the uplock block will punch up through the wing skin. Wear will occur at the uplock block hinge point (Fig. 21-9).

There is another spring in this system (Fig. 21-10). This is a lightweight spring used to position the cable when it is in the relaxed position. A canvas boot slips over the assembly and is held in position by snap fasteners. The canvas stiffens and deteriorates, allowing the boot to shift forward, sometimes to the point that it covers the end of the uplock block. This could be serious. The boot should be replaced.

CONTROL CABLES

Since the control cables play such an important part, most of us worry about their reliability, condition and their tension.

Control cable condition is something that should be checked at every annual. Accepted practice is to run a rag along the cable. If there is a broken strand, it will catch in the cloth material which makes it easy for the mechanic to detect a worn cable. Beech has used steel cables that had a built-in lubricant. This lubricant would get the factory workers' hands dirty, so they degreased the cables. This practice caused premature cable wear and cables rusted, so the factory stopped the degrease practice.

Why dosen't the factory use stainless steel cables? Well, they did consider it, but stainless steel stretches, so basic rig tension would vary. Beech pre-stretches control cables, so once they have been pre-stretched, they will not stretch farther. Cable tension is set at 70 degrees room temperature. This of course, is a place to start. In most cases, cable tension is not critical. A good example: let's say the airplane sits out in the sun at Phoenix, where it is 114 degrees in the shade. Under these conditions, the fuselage and wings will expand to a considerable degree so cable tension will be very tight. Now, let's park the airplane out-of-doors at Minneapolis where it is 40 below zero. Cables will lay loose since the overall air frame has shrunk considerably. In both extremes, the airplane flies well and the cables give no trouble.

Some owners worry about elevator trim tab cables. These cables will rust and if allowed to go long enough will finally break. There are stories that say severe flutter will occur when a cable breaks. This, however is not true. I have talked to owners who have had tab cables break and experienced absolutely no flutter.

When your Bonanza was new, the controls moved with very little friction. If given reasonable care, they should move freely throughout the airplanes life. Most cable pulleys are ball bearing mounted and are of the sealed type, so require no lubricant. There are a few pulleys that turn on bushings and these are the pulleys that can freeze up and not turn. When this happens, the control cable will cut a flat spot in the formica pulley.

There is a bellcrank located inside the wing at the aileron push-pull rod location. Access can be gained to this bellcrank through an access plate on the underneath side of the wing. Since this bellcrank is out of sight, it is seldom lubricated. Stiff aileron controls are usually caused by a binding bellcrank or a too-tight chain tension inside the throw over control arm. Usually if this chain is too tight, you can feel each chain link as it passes over each sprocket tooth. Chain tension is adjustable by turnbuckles inside the control arm. The control column is mounted on a series of nylon rollers that can be adjusted to give the most desirable feel to the pilot involved. This adjustment varies to a considerable degree. The main point: it shouldn't be set too tight. Starting with Serial D-6562 the N35 bob weight was added to the elevator cable. This weight was installed to provide feel and resistance to up elevator and is an added safety feature.

GUST LOCKS

When your Bonanza sits out-of-doors and is subjected to a strong windstorm and you forget to install gust locks, where should you look for possible damage? Well the most obvious, is a bent or wrinkled aileron or elevator. Check the condition of hinge and hinge attach points. It would be a rare case indeed, if control cable pulley attach brackets in the fuselage belly were damaged, but it wouldn't hurt to check them for condition anyway.

There is a safety feature built into gust locks on your Bonanza. It is surprising how many people try to take off with gust locks in place. If you try to do this in your Bonanza, it won't take off but it will run off the runway and out into the Boondocks which should get your attention.

WINGS

The first test model Bonanza flown had a Laminar flow wing. This was the same type airfoil used on the P-51 Mustang fighter plane. Since this wing did not perform to the satisfaction of the Beech flight test engineers, Beech selected the 23000 series airfoil. It remains the same today.

While the wing looks the same between models, the similarity ends there. The wing on Serial D-1 thru D-1500 (Model 35) was the same. The wing structure on Serials D-1501 (Model A35) thru D-2200 was modified slightly. At D-3799 (Mid E35) thru D-4251 (F35) still more changes were made.

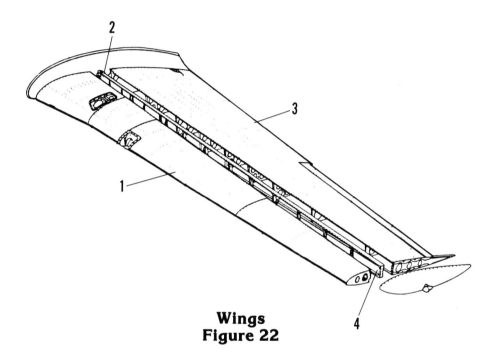

Wings
Figure 22

The wing is built in three basic sections: the leading edge (Fig. 22-1), the front spar (Fig. 22-2) and the box section (Fig. 22-3) that includes the rear spar. The wing is held together with four steel wire hinge pins. The main strength in the wing is the leading edge and the spar that form a box. The front spar leading edge structure carries the bulk of in-flight loads while the rear spar carries more of the landing load.

The front spar in airplanes prior to Serial D-4351 (Mid G35) was made up of an upper and lower spar cap. A solid web separated the spar caps, and extended from the spar root to the outboard end of the wheel well. The remaining spar consisted of vertical risers or spacers, something like 15 or so inches apart. Wing spars (Fig. 22-4) after

Serial D-4251 included a solid web from the root to the wing tip.

The wing is secured to the front and rear center section spars by four high-strength bolts. This method of wing attachment has been of some concern to owners. However, to my knowledge, there has never been an in-flight failure of these bolts. In fact, there have been landing accidents that broke a wing off completely, but wing attach bolts remained tight and undamaged.

There has been reported wing bolt failure in the King Air series. These bolts are different from the Bonanza series. But because of these known failures, the Beech Factory has called out for the following wing bolt inspection: on the Model 33, 35 and 36 Series Bonanzas; the Model 95 Travelair, the Model 55, 56 and 58 Series Barons. King Air wing bolts were of different material and design so cannot be compared to Bonanza wing bolts.

New airplanes. Inspect wing bolts at the end of 5 years, 10 years and 15 years. At 20 years, replace the bolts. After bolt replacement, repeat the inspection cycle.

Airplanes 5 years and older. Inspect the wing bolts at the first scheduled inspection. Inspect again at 5 years, 10 years and 15 years. At 20 years, replace the bolts. After bolt replacement, the inspection cycle should be repeated.

Wing bolt diameter was increased at D-1501 and was increased as airplane gross weight was increased. This change poses no problem unless a late model wing is being installed on an early model Bonanza. In this case the original size bolt is used to conform with the bolt size in the center section spar. A bushing is required in the replacement wing so that the original smaller diameter bolt can be used. The bolt holes in the top front wing spar and the upper and lower bolt holes in the rear wing spar are considerably larger than the wing bolts.

The holes in the bottom front wing spar fit relatively snug. The lower wing bolt with its snug fit acts as a hinge point so that the angle of incidence can be adjusted to fine tune rig. The looseness in fit of the top front spar bolt hole and the upper and lower wing bolt holes allows the angle of incidence of the wing to be varied.

A new airplane is normally rigged with one wing angle of incidence washed out completely and the other wing washed out halfway. This setting is changed as needed after test flights.

The aluminum forging bathtub fittings at the top of both the front and rear spar are serrated. As the wing is installed on the fuselage, soft aluminum washers are installed on the two top serrated fittings. As the wing bolts are torqued in place, these serrations cut into the aluminum washers to form a sheer joint. Any time the top wing bolts are loosened, new soft aluminum washers should be installed. After the airplane has been flown 100 hours, the wing bolts should be retorqued. This is important. Wing bolts require special wrenches built by Beech. **Do not use a substitute wrench.**

Landing lights were installed in some wing leading edges. They weakened the wing to the point that when the wing would break in flight, it would fail at this point. This is something to consider when a section of the leading edge is removed for radar installation.

Hail will, of course, damage the entire airplane, but wings and horizontal stabilizers seem to suffer the most damage. Ailerons seem to dent the most but fortunately they are symmetrical, so they can be switched from the right to left and left to right which will then position both bottom sides on top which looks better. The hail dents will still be there but they won't show. The dents won't cause trouble. In fact, they may strengthen the skin.

The right way to repair the wing skins damaged by hail is to replace the skins. Some shops will fill the dents with a filler and then repaint the wings. If they do a good job, it is hard to detect, but the added filler and paint adds weight and the filler may loosen. If you buy a previously owned airplane, look the wings over carefully for covered-up hail damage.

Bonanza wings have two degrees of twist so when replacing skins, it is best to remove rivets from one panel of skin at a time. Skins can be made up from sheet stock. It is best to buy them from Beech, as they will come with pilot holes that help in wing alignment. Wings that have been overstresssed will have skin wrinkles starting at the the front spar attach fitting. They will run diagonally outboard on the top, on the bottom wing there will be diagonal wrinkles starting at the outboard end of the wheel well. In most cases these wrinkled skins can be replaced to bring the structural strength back to normal. Skin wrinkles caused by the wing tip contacting the ground or the wing striking some object, are called spring wrinkles. This type wrinkle will deform the wing structure, but once the rivets are removed, the inner wing structure will usually return to its normal shape.

The wing leading edge sustains the most frequent damage. Let's say you hit a duck and it dents the leading edge three feet in from the tip. The correct repair is to replace the skin. But repair can be made by drilling a small hole in the center of the dent, then inserting a steel hook in the hole and pulling out the dent. Use a rolling pin to shape and to roll out the wrinkles. The rolling pin will smooth out skin without stretching it. This method of repair will not remove all the minor dents. What remains can be filled with body putty, giving the damaged area a smooth appearance.

Let's say you catch a post in the outboard section of the wing leading edge. Damage is extensive but seldom goes beyond the spar. This section of skin can be replaced without removing the leading edge from the wing. The leading edge skin rivets to an extruded hinge which in turn is attached to the spar by piano wire. In this type of repair, remove the rivets from the hinge and ribs and replace the skin and any damaged ribs. To make it possible to buck rivets after the new skin is in place, you can cut access holes in the bottom side leading edge skins and finish the holes as an inspection plate hole is finished. Blind or cherry lock rivets are an acceptable choice which would eliminate the need for the access holes.

Let's say we damage the center or inboard section leading edge skin. The entire leading edge can be removed by pulling the two wires that secure the leading edge to the spar. If the wing has been in service for several years, the removal of the steel piano wire can be a problem. A simple wire puller tool can be made that will crank the wire out. Position the base of the tool against the upper and lower spar cap. Insert the hinge wire through the hole in the shaft. Wrap the surplus wire around the shaft and crank the wire out.

An alternate tool can be made. Use a 1-3/4 inch diameter steel pipe. Drill a 1/8 inch hole 15 to 18 inches from the end of the pipe. Slip the hinge wire through the 1/8 inch hole and clamp vice grip pliers on the wire next to the pipe. Position a section of 2 X 4 wood across the front and rear spar ends. Using the pipe as a fulcrum, remove the wire. In both tools use steady pulling pressure. Avoid sudden jerks which will cause the wire to snap. It would ruin your day. Should the wire break, say, halfway down the wing spar, remove one or two hinge lugs to gain access to the wire and remove the remaining wire.

While the wing leading edge can be replaced without removing the wing, it is probably better in the long run to remove the wing from the airplane. When it is time to reinstall the leading edge, use new wires. Before inserting the wires, braze a drill bit the same diameter as the hole in the hinge, onto the hinge pin. Run the drill bit through both hinges. This will clear the hinge of debris and will straighten out any misalignment. Remove the drill bit and radius the end of the hinge wire. Use Beech Kit 35-588 which has telescoping rods that hold the wire rigid and drive the wire in position with an E-2 rivet gun. Tap on the hinge as the point of the wire progresses down the hinge. If you reach a point where the wire simply refuses to move, remove three or four rivets from the hinge at the wire point. This will allow the hinge to shift a few thousandths and the wire will move on in. The rivets can be replaced with cherry locks.

Wing tips are mostly cosmetic. Some owners install M35 wing tips on their earlier models. I get mixed reports. Some say they increase speed, others say they lose speed. The shape of the outboard wing end has not changed so any of the several designed wing tips will fit.

WING FLAP

When a system works as well as the wing flaps on your Bonanza, the mechanics who inspect the airplane tend to overlook the system. Sure, they extend and retract the flaps but how often do they inspect the motor brushes or lubricant in the actuators or flex drive shaft? We

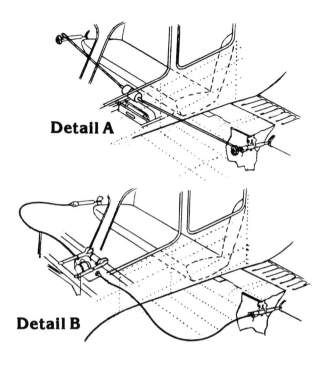

Detail A

Detail B

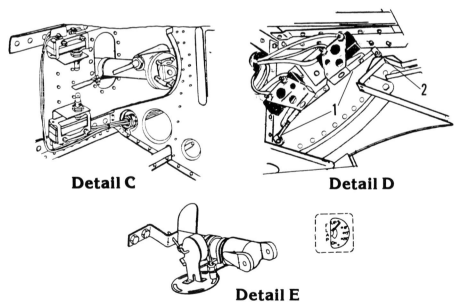

Detail C

Detail D

Detail E

Wing Flaps
Figure 23

have included schematics so that ypu can see how the system works. In the Model 35 Serial D-1 thru D-838 (Fig. 23-A) the flap motor and gearbox were located on the rear center section spar. Steel drive rods were routed outboard to the flap actuators. Replacement parts for this flap system are almost nonexistent. The only source of supply is aircraft salvage yards.

Starting with airplane Serial D-839 (Fig. 23-B), the flap motor was moved to the front center section spar, and flexible drive shafts were routed to the flap actuators. This basic system remains today. Flap limit switches (Fig. 23-C) on airplane Serial D-1 thru D-3701 (mid E35) were mounted on ribs inside the left wing and are accessible through the left wheel well. These limit switches were protected from weather but were fairly hard to adjust.

Flap travel on Serial D-1 to D-2200 (B35) was 20 degrees. While it is not legal, flap travel on some of these airplanes has been extended to 30 degrees.

Starting with airplane Serial D-3702 (mid E35) (Fig. 23-D), flap limit switches were mounted on a bracket and installed on the outboard side of the inboard flap track in the left wing panel. This location makes the switches more accessible, but it also exposes them to weather.

A steel spring actuating arm and roller (Fig. 23-D1) is actuated by a cam (Fig. 23-D2) that is part of the flap. The roller on the acutator spring should have a drop of oil, say, once a year.

Once in a long while, a wing flap may fail to retract. Usually, you can reach in and flip the limit switch actuator arm and the flap will retract. If the flap will not extend because of a stuck limit switch, you will have to disconnect the left flap drive cable at the flap motor and turn the shaft by hand to extend the left flap, to gain access to the stuck limit switch. If your airplane serial falls between D-1 and D-3701 (E35) you can gain access to both limit switches through the left wheel well.

Wing flaps are relatively trouble free. An observant owner may notice with some alarm that one flap inboard trailing edge extends below the fuselage belly while the flap on the other wing may be flush with the fuselage belly. This is as it should be, because wing angle of incidence is different in each wing and may vary from airplane to airplane. So it is nothing to be alarmed about.

Sometimes when an airplane flies slightly wing heavy, the mechanic may lower one flap to raise the heavy wing rather than rotate a wing which is the correct way, but much more difficult to do.

The left wing flap controls both flaps' travel since the flap limit switches are secured to the left wing. A cam arrangement built into the left flap controls not only the up-and-down travel, but the approach limit found on the V35, Serial D-7977 and after.

Flaps should be rigged to extend the same degree of travel when extending. They should both stop at the same time when in the retract position. This is easy to determine. Move the flap trailing edge up and down to detect looseness. Let's say that when you make this test you find you can detect considerable looseness in the left flap, but when you check the right flap there is absolutely no movement. In this situation, the right flap rollers have reached the end of the slots in the flap tracks before the left flap cams have actuated the up-limit switch. When this condition exists, it means that the flex flap actuator drive shaft is wrapping up, which overloads the shaft and could cause it to fail. What would happen if this cable would break when the flap reached is up-travel? Well, the next time you extended flaps, the right flap would remain in the retract position and the left flap would extend. This condition would get your attention but your Bonanza is fully controllable.

What should you do to correct this?

Uneven travel in the retract position can be corrected by one of several methods. First, determine if the flap is rigged too tight to the wing. Probably the best way to check this is to actuate the flaps and to listen to the flap motor and the flap motor coast. If the motor labors or if there is little or no coast, the flap is rigged too tight. This condition can be corrected by extending the flaps. Remove the bolt in the flap actuator and where it attaches to the actuator bracket on the flap, turn the actuator out to lengthen one-half turn. The right-hand actuator has left-hand threads and the left-hand actuator has right-hand threads. If the right-hand actuator is rigged about right, then you can adjust the left flap tighter by removing the single bolt in the flap actuator end and screwing the actuator one-half turn.

After adjusting the left flap to match the right flap and the airplane flies left-wing heavy, you will know the flap was rigged loose to correct for wing heavy. So lengthen the actuator one-half turn and then add rubber bumpers to take out looseness at the trailing edge. Flaps were originally rigged so that the rollers would just barely touch the end of the flap tracks. Then rubber bumpers were cemented in the tracks to provide a firm fit in the retract position. The only problem with this design was that the rubber bumpers were forever falling out. Starting with Serial D-7750 (S35), a different design flap bumper was installed. This was essentially a doorstop bumper. It consisted of a rubber cap on a threaded machine screw that screwed into an anchor nut, riveted to a small rib flange which was part of the wing trailing edge.

This bumper can be adjusted to make rubber contact with the flap leading edge at its outboard end. It can be installed on any model and is quite satisfactory. The rubber cap will crack with service but it is easy to replace. Flap actuators should be lubricated every 1000 hours and according to the manual, rebuilt or replaced every 2000 hours.

Unless the actuator leaks grease, there is really not much reason to change grease at 1000 hours. If it does leak, it can easily be detected by extending the flaps and observing the extended flap actuator shaft.

If the shaft is coated with oil, then it is a good idea to have the actuator removed, disassembled, cleaned, inspected and the Garlock and "O" ring seals replaced. You probably won't find parts worn but if you do, the worn parts should be replaced. Wear can sometimes be detected in flap actuators by extending the flaps halfway and by lifting up on the flap trailing edge. Observe the area where the jack screw shaft exits the actuator. If internal wear is present, the actuator will flex up and down as pressure on the flap is applied. If flexing indicates wear, the actuator should be disassembled.

I won't go into disassembly of the actuator since it is covered in the maintenance manual. If you should do the work yourself, remember the snap ring that holds the actuator together must be installed with the sharp edge against pressure.

Starting with Serial D-7977 (V35), a flap position indicator was added (Fig. 23-E). The indicator is activated by a rheostat that is secured to the left flap actuator. This rheostat can be adjusted to make the instrument on the panel read correctly.

Those of you who do not have a flap position indicator—your flaps can be marked with a strip of tape so that you can see the tape from the pilot's seat. Use a bubble protractor to determine when the flap has reached 15 degrees and while you sit in the pilot's seat, have someone position the tape until you can just see the tape past the wing trailing edge. Follow the same procedure to locate 20-degree position.

Each flap moves on four rollers that roll in the flap tracks. These rollers have a flange on one side. This flange holds the roller in the track but its important function is to space the flap in the track. The roller flange should always be on the inside of both tracks, like the flange on railroad car wheels. Flap rollers should be lubricated occasionally. Silicone spray is an ideal lubricant since it is slick and it won't collect dirt.

Flaps on early Bonanzas, Serial D-1 thru D-3950 (E35) were made of magnesium. Flaps on D-3951 and after are aluminum and have a single spar. The curved area forward of the spar gives it its structural strength. It is a good idea to inspect the skin around the flap actuator attach point. If the skin in this area is wrinkled or deformed, it means that the two support bulkheads below the attach bracket are cracked. The right-hand flap is reinforced in the wing walk area with a corrugated stiffener.

Wing flaps and their support brackets are strong. Jack screws are also strong. In an emergency, don't be afraid to use your flaps to slow down. Flaps in full extension position create about the same amount of drag as landing gear in the extended position.

Wing flaps have a dual purpose. They slow the airplane in flight and aid in lift. 15 degrees of flap should be used during landing approach to aid in keeping engine temperature normal. They should be extended 10 degrees for soft field take off, 15 degrees for short field take off and 20 degrees for obstacle take off.

Let's see how flaps aid in take off. As Bonanza flaps are extended, they move aft. This increases wing lifting area. As the flap moves aft, the trailing edge moves down. This movement creates a venturi-type gap between the wing trailing edge and the flap leading edge. A venturi is a device that accepts a high volume of air but reduces it in size to squeeze the volume of air passing through. Then the area again expands to allow the volume of air to escape under reduced pressure.

The Bonanza flap leading edge is shaped like a wing leading edge, so in a partial or full extended position, it will provide lift and fly. Due to the venturi action of the gap created by the flap moving aft and down, airflow is speeded up and is moving faster than the air flowing over the wing. This high-speed flow of air passing over the airfoil section of the flap causes the flap to fly before the wing flies. This, of course, adds lift, helping the airplane to break ground sooner.

For obstacle take off, use 20-degree flaps. We want to gain altitude quickly in this case. There is one little-known stipulation for 20-degree flaps: the runway should be smooth and hard. Oh yes, keep the nose high.

For short field take off, use 15-degree flap. We don't worry about obstacles, just get the airplane off the ground. Once airborne, drop the nose to build airspeed. Soft field take off, such as a wet sod field, use 10-degree flap. In this case, we want the additional lift but we don't need the drag of too much flap extension since we already have built-in drag from the soft field. Once airborne, drop the nose slightly to build airspeed.

GAP STRIPS

Gap strips, to seal off the gap between flap and aileron to the wing, are popular vendor items. This is nothing new to Bonanza, remember the first Model 35 had spring-loaded gap strips. The springs gave trouble, so they were changed to a fixed strip. The Beech Factory felt that they were not needed and took them off. From reports, most owners think that they do improve performance at take off and landing.

Since the gap strips often make physical contact with the control surface, ice could cause them to lock up a control. So far, there have been just a few reports of this.

RUBBER FAIRINGS

Wing root fairings, stabilizer and fin root fairings are rubber extrusions that slip over the end of the root skin. These fairings are positioned in place before the wing stabilizer or fin is positioned on the fuselage. This means that to replace the fairing, the surface must be removed from the fuselage.

DZUS FASTENERS

The small dzus fasteners used on the early Bonanza engine compartment Serial D-1 thru D-4576 side panels are hard to find but Beech still stocks these parts. Order these Part No's.: 99871-CO98 receptacle, 1301765-SR09 stud, and 99785-2 pin. The dzus fastener used in the main fuel sump door in the left fuselage belly 98-2-MS spring, 98-FM-2-5 stud and 31-804-100 pin.

FUSELAGE

The Bonanza fuselage is made up of six basic parts. This is important to know should it become necessary to do extensive repair.

The six basic parts are (Fig. 24-1): **lower nacelle** or **engine compartment.** It includes the nose bug, the keel, that part that supports the engine and the cowl doors. **The cabin section** is built in two parts (Fig. 24-2), the upper and lower sections (Fig. 24-3). The cabin section includes the firewall and basically extends to the cabin rear closure bulkhead (Fig. 24-4). The **aft fuselage** (Fig. 24-5) is one piece and mates to the assembled cabin section. During assembly, the **top cabin section** is mated to the **lower cabin section.** When assembled, this section of the fuselage contains longerons (Fig. 24-6) that help support the engine compartment. It includes both the front (Fig. 24-7) and rear center section spars.

On the Model 36 Series, the lower section of the cabin section was shifted aft ten inches which, in effect, shifted the center of gravity aft ten inches. While it is not widely publicized, the structure in the top cabin section has sufficient strength to support the weight of the airplane. This fact is of little consequence to you unless you put your airplane on its back, then this built-in strength becomes very important.

On some airplanes, the cabin door does not fair in well with the windshield post. In most cases, the poor cabin door is blamed for this misfit, when in fact, the windshield post was mispositioned when the top cabin section was mated to the bottom section. Don't replace the cabin door, the new door won't fit any better. It is hard to say, but just live with the misfit.

The aft fuselage section is built in one piece and includes the structure that supports the tail section. In the "V" tail, these are two heavy bulkheads (Fig. 24-8). In the straight tails, the structure is the same, but uses a stub spar in addition. On assembly, the assembled cabin section is positioned in a mating jig where the aft fuselage is mated to the cabin section.

The nose section is mounted on a fixture which is mounted on wheels that run on a track. This fixture positions the fuselage nose section to the fuselage section where all the sections are riveted together

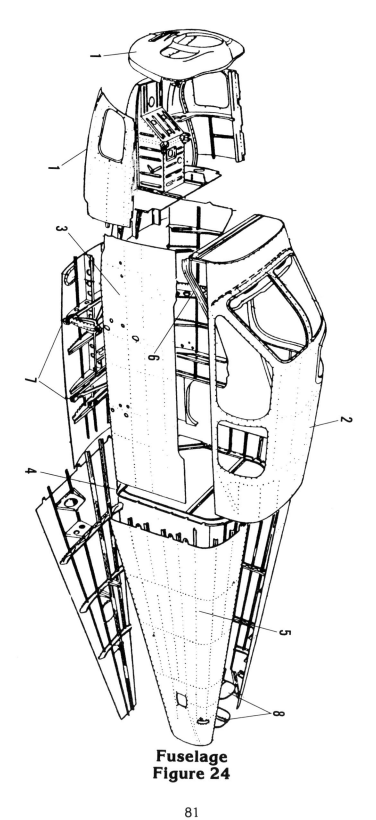

Fuselage
Figure 24

to make up the fuselage. Since the nose section moves on tracks, tolerances cannot be controlled as closely as other parts. As a result, **cowl doors** are made oversize and are trimmed to fit that particular fuselage.

What this means is that cowl doors are *not* interchangeable. If you buy a used door, chances are it won't fit. Beech tooling is excellent. This is important since most airframe parts include "pilot" holes that make perfect alignment possible, both in the factory and in the field.

Building the fuselage in sections is important to you, for in the event of serious structural damage, the damaged section can be replaced as a unit. Thanks to Beech quality tooling, such sections will align perfectly without the need of alignment tools. There is still another important advantage, **downtime.** If individual parts are ordered, there is always the chance wrong parts are ordered or parts back ordered. So when major damage occurs, replace by section.

If you have a Baron, the Bonanza and Baron fuselage are identical in shape, except the Baron has a nose baggage compartment instead of an engine compartment. The basic fuselage shape has remained the same throughout the years, but there are, in fact, considerable differences. For example, stabilizer bulkheads have been made stronger and skins have been made thicker starting with the C35. These changes came about as the airplanes' gross weight was increased. Due to the cost of new parts, it is always best to find the desired section from a like model or newer model, never an older one. When switching parts from one model to another, talk to your local FAA before you buy parts. A clear understanding can save hours of hassle later.

Bonanza Model 35 (D-1 thru 1500) used steel tubular center section spars. After years of service, this type spar was prone to crack. The steel spars were heat treated so if a crack appeared, no repair was possible. Spar reinforcement kits which strengthened the spar were made available by vendors. These kits could be used only if the steel spar was not cracked. These reinforcement kits are no longer available. As a result of the limited spar cracking, the FAA imposed rather rigid inspection procedures that included X-ray and magnaflux inspections. As time goes on, the equipment to perform these required inspections is becoming increasingly scarce. In the event a spar is found cracked, the only alternative left is to replace the spar with the later model sheet metal spar. At one time, the Beech Factory offered a replacement spar kit. A sheet metal center section spar can be purchased from the factory but the cost, compared to the value of the airplane, is prohibitive. The only alternative is to buy a sheet metal spar from a wrecked Bonanza. To replace the steel spar, again contact your local FAA office to clear paper work before attempting the change. Don't expect help from the factory in the way of blueprints or technical data. It will require 250 man-hours labor. As long as the fuselage must be opened up, it is wise to replace both center section spars.

To change spars, remove both wings. Make a long template and drill locating holes in the template to match the wing attach bolt holes in both spars. Make a template for both sides of the fuselage. Extend the template, both forward and aft and make locating attach points on the fuselage. This is necessary to establish the replacement spar position in the fuselage. Next, remove the left side fuselage skin and stringers and slip the old spars out and the new spars in place. When buying a Model 35, it would be wise to have the center section spars inspected first.

We talked about the fuselage having six parts. We included the **nacelle** or nose section, the **cowl doors,** the **upper** and **lower cabin,** the **aft fuselage** and **tail cone.** Tail cones are more or less cosmetic and they are interchangeable among the models.

Windshields and side windows have changed and the fixed long third window can be added. This can be obtained in kit form. The original windshield was two-piece and while not as pretty as the one-piece model, it was probably stronger. It is amazing how the one-piece windshield gives better vision.

The long slope windshield has at least two distinct advantages. First, it will increase airspeed by several miles per hour. Second, because it calls for a new glareshield, it gives a much-needed access to the back side of the instrument panel. It is wise to install a thicker glass to strengthen the windshield. The thicker the glass, the quieter the cabin. Remember, the thicker the glass, the more weight it adds, so don't go overboard.

The Beech-furnished windshield has a distinct advantage over vendor-furnished glass. The Beech glass is bonded to a metal frame and the frame is riveted to the fuselage. The vendor-furnished glass is just as good a quality but the holes must be drilled through the glass which can be a starting point for cracks. The vendor windshield requires a separate strip to fair the fuselage and glass together. Sometimes this fairing is not very attractive. The glareshields are similar. Generally speaking, the Beech-furnished glareshield looks best.

Keep M.E.K. or lacquer thinner away from windshield or side window glass. These chemicals will cause the glass (lucite) to craze. Incidentally, Beech windshields carry a five-year warranty.

The pilot's side new window, with its storm window that opens in, is a good improvement and will interchange with all models. The vendor-furnished cabin door window that includes the storm window that opens in, is also a good addition. Tinted glass has its advantages but not at night.

TAIL TIE DOWN RING

The tail tie down ring is supposed to be used to secure the aft fuselage when the airplane is tied down out-of-doors. Some owners with hangars want to tow the airplane tail first into the hangar. In most cases the hangar floor is uneven, so the airplane is hard to move. The tie down ring that is secured to the aft fuselage belly can be used as an attach point for a winch rope. The aircraft structure is sufficient for such towing as long as there is no shoulder to cross and the winch exerts a steady pull, "no jerks." It is not recommended that the airplane be moved backwards on anything but the hangar floor.

ENGINE COWLING

Engine cowl doors get damaged and wear out. New doors are expensive, so owners usually look for used doors.

Cowl doors are individually fit at the factory. Generally speaking, Bonanza structure is held to close tolerances, but cowl doors are the exception. If they fall within one-fourth inch, they are close, so if you find a used cowl door that will fit your airplane you are lucky. Usually cowl doors wear where they contact the nose bug. On new airplanes, the factory applies a plastic coating. This coating wears thin, so the easiest chafe material to use is plastic electrical tape or the reinforced packaging tape. Tape to the nose bug or cowl door flange. Cowl doors that are held closed by dzus fasteners are a pain in the neck, but they fit more securely and generally show less wear than the newer cowl doors that are secured by the single latch handle.

The single latch handle is fairly sensitive to adjustment. In fact, there have been cases where the latch has released the door in flight. Fortunately, the released door will open slightly and will fly there fairly steady. It gets your attention but you won't lose your door.

There is a cowl door back-up plate on the engine compartment that supports the lower cowl door edge. On some V35 Bonanzas, the forward ten inches of this back-up strip were omitted. The loss of this back-up caused the cowl door to wear rapidly. This condition still exists on many V35 Bonanzas. A fix was worked out to correct this situation and is covered by Beech Service Instruction 0439-242.

Cowl doors are well built. The inner stiffener is spot welded to the outer skin so it is strong, but hard to repair. A good mechanic can trim away the worn edge flange and bond a new flange in place.

Some owners with dzus fastener-type cowl doors want to install the new single-fastener latch. Of course anything is possible but at this time Beech does not offer a kit, so you would have to buy individual parts. My advice is to stick with your dzus fasteners.

Here are some dzus fastener part numbers:

Serial D-1 thru D-5330

1301762SF-09	Stud
130175-2PO98	Spring
99871-C-098	Receptacle
295846-1	Grommet
99785-2	Pin

Serial D-5331 thru D-6161 using
35-410020-14 & -15 cowl doors
same as above

Serial D-6162 thru D-9068 using
35410460-5 & -6 doors

98265-1-120	Stud
295250-5	Grommet
130175-5P-098	Receptacle

Engine compartment side panels dzus fasteners are becoming increasingly hard to find. At this time Beech still stocks the parts.

For Bonanzas Serial D-1 thru D-4576 order:

99871-C-098	Receptacle
1301765SR09	Stud
99785-2	Pin

On Bonanzas Serial D-4577 and after order:

98264-1-090	Stud
99871-2	Pin
295846-1	Grommet

Cracks may appear in the lower right-hand corner of the nose bug pan on those models with a relief cut-out. Cracks often appear in the side keel panel where the slanting portion of the keel changes to horizontal. A stop-drilled hole will usually stop crack progression. Sometimes a doubler patch is needed to stop the side keel cracks from progressing.

On occasion the nose bug pan has cracked at the point that the induction hose adapter attaches to the nose bug pan. In order to see these cracks, the induction air filter must be removed.

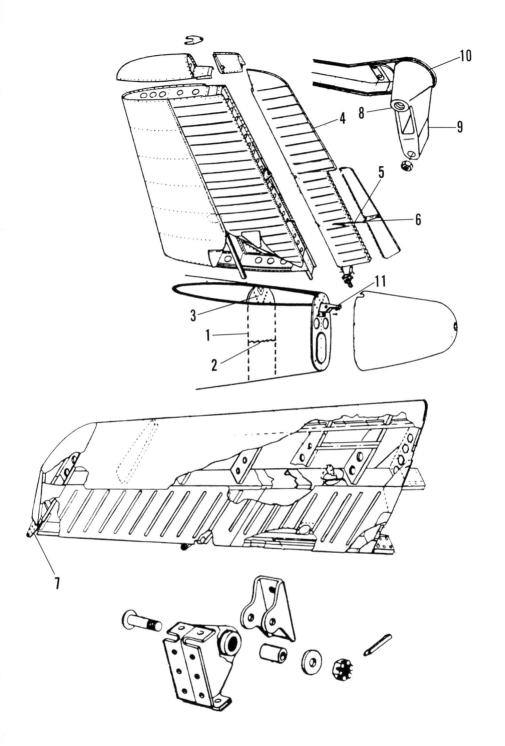

Tail Section
Figure 25

TAIL SECTION

When you think of Bonanzas, you think of "V" tails. This unique tail design has set this fine airplane apart from the crowd. I think the Germans used it first. Beech tried it out on a modified AT-10 and on their twin Quad, a four-engine commuter-type airplane. The tail worked so well that they put it on the Bonanza. The "V" tail has some distinct advantages. It is lighter, and gives less drag, making it more efficient. While the "V" tail, on all models, looks similar, that is where the similarity ends. The stabilizer cord was made wider starting with the Model C35. As engine horsepower was increased, the angle of incidence was also changed to compensate for the increase in engine torque. There were slight internal changes made, mainly the addition of a stringer to the leading skin forward of the front spar. In the Model 35 thru the B35, the stabilizer spar was attached to a magnesium casting, which in turn was secured to a bulkhead in the fuselage. After years of service, and on an airplane with 17,000 hours, this magnesium casting was found to be cracked. Everyone was caught by surprise, for to this point, there were no reports of casting cracks. The FAA ordered all castings inspected. Many were found cracked but in areas that would not affect structural integrity.

Beech had no castings in stock so they machined parts from solid aluminum stock. The stabilizer attach bulkhead (Fig. 25-1) in the fuselage of the Model 35 and A35 was a single-thickness part. This was structurally sound for normal flight loads, but if someone were to chin themselves by hanging on to the stabilizer tip or bang the stabilizer against the "T" hangar wall, it could crack the stabilizer attach bulkhead in the fuselage (Fig. 25-2). Once this bulkhead cracks, the stabilizer will flex at an alarming rate. This condition has not changed through the years, so this particular bulkhead should be inspected for buckles and cracks.

Starting with the B35, this particular bulkhead was doubled by adding a second bulkhead back to back and the fuselage skin in the area of the bulkhead was thickened.

Starting with the C35, the stabilizer cord was widened and the stabilizer spar was bolted directly to the fuselage bulkhead (Fig. 25-3). This method of attachment remains today.

The stabilizer angle of incidence has been changed several times on the "V" tail mainly due to engine horsepower changes. Starting with the Model S35, the left elevator horn rides above the stabilizer tip when in normal cruise flight. This is as it should be.

The Model 33 and 36 series stabilizers mount at a different angle of incidence. Elevators on the Model 35 series and Model 33 and 36 are similar, in that they all have magnesium skins (Fig. 25-4). The trim tabs on the Model 35 are cable actuated (Fig. 25-5). This system has been criticized but has, by and large, given less trouble than the mechanical tab actuator system used on the Model 33, 36 or Barons.

Smaller diameter cables were used on the Model 35 thru the G35. Starting with the H35, cable size and trim tab cord were increased. There are three primary factors that contribute to cable failure. Number one is rust. Unproptected cables rust. Beech does not use stainless steel cables, I'm told, because stainless steel cables stretch.

Cable tension is the number two factor. Some trim tab cables are rigged tight as a fiddle string, which overloads pulleys and trim tab horns.

Number three, the clevis bolt (Fig. 25-6) at the trim tab horn is over-torqued. The clevis bolt torque should be low enough that the bolt can be turned by hand. When the clevis bolt is too tight, the clevis becomes rigid on the tab horn. As the trim tab is moved, all movement of the cable occurs at the ferrel end of the clevis causing a concentration of bend which makes the cable fail. Contrary to some rumors, the Model 35 trim tab will not flutter if the trim tab cable breaks in flight. If the elevators are out of balance, this could occur. However, I know of reported cases of a "V" tail Bonanza taking off and flying 100 miles with a broken trim tab cable.

On the Model 33 and 36 series, accumulated tolerances in the trim tab actuator components add up to considerable free movement at the trim tab trailing edge. I would think one-quarter inch total travel of the tab trailing edge would not be excessive. The Model 35 trim tabs had no contour but the Model A35 thru the G35 used a tab contour on the bottom side of the tab. On the H35 and after, contour was on the top side. It is not uncommon to find tabs on the Model A35 thru the G35 installed upside down. More frequently, the trim tab hinge wires are installed wrong. When the trim hinge wire on these models is installed correctly, the trim tab is held away from the elevator hinge bulkhead by the hinge wire.

The outboard hinge bearing (Fig. 25-7) on all the model 35, 33 and 36 elevators will wear more rapidly than the other two bearings. End play in the inboard hinge bearing (Fig. 25-8) should be controlled with washer shims. The elevator horn (Fig. 25-9) should be inspected for cracks and for security with the elevator structure (Fig. 25-10). The inboard elevator bearing support casting (Fig. 25-11) should also be inspected for cracks and security.

Elevator balance is essential. It is astounding how many elevators are flying out of balance. Elevators on the Model 33 and 36 Series, to my knowledge, have not fluttered, but it is a possibility if they are out of balance. Ruddervators on the Model 35 series have fluttered but only in cases where they were out of balance. Contrary to some beliefs, flutter does not occur at high airspeeds. It does occur as the airplane is slowed down and just prior to touchdown. In such cases, flutter is violent to the extent it will cause severe damage to the aft fuselage. It is paint shops or uninformed mechanics who touch up paint or add patches to elevator skins that put them out of balance.

Elevators balance heavy on the trailing edge, so if you lose patches of paint from the elevator, it will not adversely affect balance.

When it is time to repaint elevators, here is what you do. Remove the elevators from the stabilizer. Strip off the old paint. The elevator skin will be brown in color. If it's necessary to sand the surface, and it probably will be, then it should be washed in Dow 19 or Dowtreat. You can make this solution by mixing 1-1/3 oz. of dry chromic acid with 1 oz. of calcium sulfate and one gallon of water.

Wash the elevator in this solution. Rinse with water. Dry the surface thoroughly. Suspend the elevator by its trailing edge. You are now ready to apply a light even coat of Epoxy primer. Once the primer is thoroughly dry, apply the color coat. Balance the surface according to specs in the Beech Maintenance Manual.

Beech Service Bulletin No. 0989 calls for inspection of the elevator push pull rods for internal condition. This is a one-time inspection and should be accomplished. Remove one rod at a time. Measure the overall length. Remove the rod ends. Sight through the rod. If O.K., fill with cosmolene and reinstall the rod ends to the overall measured length. Wrap a strip of black tape around the tube to designate inspection conformity. Do not mix the rods. They are not the same length.

G33 STABILIZERS

Some owners of Model G33 Bonanzas may notice that one horizontal stabilizer droops as much as 1-1/2 inches at the tip. In other words one stabilizer extends 90 degrees to the fuselage side while the opposite side stabilizer may extend 92 degrees. Still the airplane rigs out in good shape and flies well. This droop is the result of an error in tooling at the factory. They did, in fact, mislocate the stabilizer on the stud spar. Normally you wouldn't notice this droop and it really doesn't hurt anything. I don't know how many airplanes were involved, perhaps 10 to 25. I doubt if even Beech knows. In all probability the condition could be corrected by installing a new sub spar in the fuselage, but it isn't necessary.

CABIN DOOR

The cabin door is one of the most important parts of your Bonanza. If the cabin door doesn't work right when you get into the cabin, chances are nothing else will work right either. The cabin door gets blamed for poor fit when it is, in fact, the door opening of the fuselage that is off. Tooling for the cabin door is exact, making the door shape consistent. Cabin door frames prior to somewhere around the Model

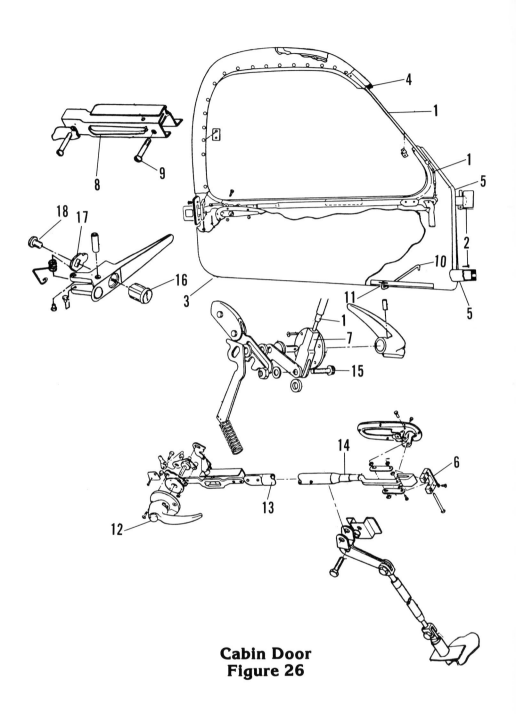

Cabin Door
Figure 26

V35 were made in two pieces. When the change was made, a one-piece door frame was used.

The door latching mechanism is installed in the frame first. It includes a teleflex cable (Fig. 26-1) that connects to the inside cabin latch actuator mechanism to the top latch in the cabin door. This cable lays inside and fastens to the door frame.

In defense of the design engineers, they spot weld the door's skin to the door frame to insure rigidity but it covers the cable which ruins the mechanic's day if he must work on the latching mechanism.

Two types of door hinges are used (Fig. 26-2). The internal hinge is inside the fuselage to make the fuselage area free of obstructions. Hinge pins are located in a hard-to-get-to place. They are held in position by a right-angle clip, positioned over the head of the hinge pin and are held in place by a single sheet metal screw. The top hinge pin installs from bottom to top and the lower from top to bottom. It is necessary to remove the glove box and upholstered side panel to get to the door hinge pins. A second hinge known as the 90-degree hinge is used. This is a stronger hinge but it does extend into the airstream. This hinge is favored by operators who need to get large objects through the cabin door opening.

Loads on the cabin doors are quite heavy. As airspeeds increased, a third latch point was added (Fig. 26-3) to the bottom aft door to prevent it from sucking open in the lower aft corner. The door along the windshield post will also move outboard when airspeeds increase (Fig. 26-4). The door will also shift aft and down under high loads. In some Model 58 Barons, it was necessary to add an index pin in the windshield portion of the door to prevent the door from moving outboard and to shim up under the third latch pin to prevent the door from shifting down. If a door can shift in the door opening due to worn hinge pins, improper adjustment or air loads, it will be impossible to seal the door from air leaks. Impossible may be a bit strong. The new, vendor-furnished, inflatable seal will do the job.

As a rule, mechanics are afraid of cabin doors, only because they do not know how to adjust them. The door hinges are adjustable at the door frame (Fig. 26-5). Shims can be used under the hinge to help position the door. The aft door latch (Fig. 26-6) is adjustable and positions the lower half of the door. We talked earlier of a teleflex cable inside the forward door frame. This cable actuates the top door latch. The top door latch differs by model but basically retracts into the door, then moves out as the door latch catch moves back into the cabin door and pulls the top half of the door to the fuselage. As you rotate the inside door latch, you should feel a distinct snap. This snap is the top door latch breaking past a cam lock that prevents the top cabin door from opening in flight. In order to tighten the top portion of the cabin door to the fuselage, some mechanics will shorten the adjustment on the teleflex cable (Fig. 26-7). The purpose of the teleflex cable is to actuate the door latch through its travel range. When the adjustment is shortened beyond the top latch travel, it overstresses the teleflex cable, causing it to break. The top latch pin in the top fuselage door frame varies in design but basically can be moved in or out by adding or removing washers. The current production pin (Fig. 26-8; (K35 & after) is adjusted by screwing in or out on the forward Phillips head machine screw (Fig. 26-9). In airplane Serials D-3226 thru D-5726, the door latch pin was mounted in a casting that had a total of six holes drilled in the casting to accommodate the latch pin. There were six holes in the top side of the casting and six on the bottom side. The latch pin fits into two of these holes. In order to adjust the pin fore and aft, the pin could be positioned in any one of the front three holes. If that did not position the pin correctly, the casting could be rotated to give three more location choices. The casting can be adjusted in or out with washers.

The door opening frame in the fuselage slopes outward so the top latch casting slopes out at the top with the latch pin centered in the casting. The latch pin is canted outboard at the top. When the top latch contacts the latch pin near its bottom end and then airloads are imposed on the door, the door latch will slide up the latch pin. Since the latch pin is canted out at the top, the tension on the door latch will loosen and the top door will leak air. New holes should be drilled, so that even with the casting position at, say, 30 degrees in the fuselage, the latch pin would be vertical so that when the latch moves up, latch tension is the same.

Since the cabin door covers a sizeable hole in the fuselage, a door-stop (Fig. 26-10) is used. It prevents the door from opening too far and holds it open. This chrome-plated rod is heat treated and very hard and strong. It extends into a hole in the door-jamb in the fuselage. In some early Bonanzas, the door-stop was inserted in holes in the sheet metal frame and was held in place with a cotter key. Newer versions have the rod inserted in a rubber bushing so they will lift out. There is a pin through the door end of the door-stop rod (Fig. 26-11). In order to free the door end of the rod, simply open the door until the pin in the door-stop rod is parallel with the opening in the door track, push down on the rod to clear the door, then open the door farther.

There is a steel track inside the door that the door-stop rod slides in. This track gets rough which makes the door open hard and makes the stop rod slide hard. This steel track is held in place with rivets. It can be removed by drilling out the attach rivets and widening the slot in the door-frame enough to remove the track. The new track can be slipped inside the door and secured with blind rivets. The inside door handle on the early Bonanzas had a tab (Fig. 26-12) that had to be compressed to unlock the door latch. This handle was superceded by a push button handle. The later model handle can be used on the earlier doors. Order Part No. 95-380010 handle and 35-40464 shaft.

The inside door handle connects to the back latch by a rod (Fig. 26-13). The brass aft latch screws into the rod so can be adjusted (Fig. 26-14). The rear latch plate is also adjustable. When adjusting these latches, it is best to disconnect the top latch (Fig. 26-15), then adjust the rear latch. This will position the lower two-thirds of the door, then adjust the top latch.

In case the teleflex cable should break, disconnect the cable at the top and bottom end. Drill off the heads of two machine screws that hold the cable in position in the door. Stuff a cloth in the door below the teleflex cable to catch the residue. Attach a strong wire to the top end of the cable, secure the wire below the brazed-on collar. Pull the broken teleflex cable out from the top of the door. Make up two steel clamps that will hold the replacement cable in place. Fit the lower clamp between the two brazed on collars. Position the clamp so it will lay flush with the inside door frame. Braze on a 6/32 steel nut to both clamps, to provide threads to the attach bolts. Position the lower clamp to the cable. Attach a strong piece of wire to the top collar and wrap the wire around the cable so it will guide the cable. Disconnect the cabin door hold-open rod and open the door wide. Insert the strong wire from the bottom side of the forward door, followed by the teleflex cable. Pull the teleflex cable in position. Work the previously installed lower clamp in position and secure with a 6/32 machine screw. Slip the second clamp on the top end of the teleflex cable, and work in position and secure with a 6/32 machine screw. Hook up the teleflex cable.

The outside door handle is operated by the rear latch link rod that connects to the inside handle. If the outside handle does not tuck into the recessed adapter, it is because the rear latch is not adjusted properly or the rod from the inside door latch is adjusted too short.

The cabin door lock plug frequently gives trouble (Fig. 26-16). The main reason it falls out of the door is because someone tries to open the door when it is locked. The lock plug has a square shoulder on its inboard end. A locking tab (Fig. 26-17) fits on this square end. On airplanes prior to the H35, the lock plug locking tab was held in position by swaging or spinning the square lock plug end. This method of securing the lock tab would withstand an 80-pound pull on the outside door handle which is not hard to exceed. An improvement was made that used a special screw (Fig. 26-18) to hold the tab in place. There isn't much room so a special, gound-down short-thread bolt is required, which you can make yourself.

If you must replace the door lock plug, you can use your old key by inserting the key in the plug. While in the unlocked position, file off any protruding tumblers. This way, you don't have to carry an extra key.

SKIN CANNING

Once in a while you will find a normally quiet Bonanza that will suddenly start making a strange sound. This sound can be a simple buzz or it can sound like a twin engine airplane with the props out of sync. It can even sound like the muffler has suddenly fallen off. There have been some cases where it was described as vibration in the airframe.

The trouble is indeed vibration but it is a panel of skin vibrating or buzzing. Usually this condition will start when the airplane attitude changes, such as a climb, or when leveling off after a climb. The noise can sometimes be stopped by changing power setting or airplane's attitude.

Outside temperature has some effect, since on a hot day aircraft skin will expand causing canning that won't appear on a normal day.

You may notice a skin panel, perhaps between stringers, working or canning on the top side of either wing. This is common and more or less natural. On some airplanes, you can hear a popping sound as you taxi. This is usually caused by skin canning on the lower nose bug, close to the area of the nose strut hinge bolt. On some new Bonanzas you can see angle stiffeners inside the nose bug in this area. It means this canning was noted before the airplane was delivered. If you encounter this condition, install a ½ X ½ inch stiffener to the inside area. It is best to rivet the stiffener in place but it can be bonded with epoxy. The access panel below the landing gear gearbox will sometimes set up quite a buzz. This can be stopped by adding an angle stiffener or sound deadener to the inside panel.

A sound like a twin engine airplane with the props out of sync is caused by skin on the lower side of the wing located aft of the rear spar. Sometimes if the wing flap is rigged too tight in the retract position, it will cause this vibration. If this is the case, it is easy to prove by just barely extending the wing flaps. If the noise goes away, the flaps are rigged too tight. However, it could be caused by the way the skin was formed during manufacture and not a too-tight flap rig situation. This can be corrected by extending the flaps to provide room to work, then by hand forming the skin to give a slight curve to the skin. Angle stiffener can be added at ten-inch spacing to stop the skin buzzing.

There is an area in the fuselage just below and inboard of the wing that might can. It is usually on the right side. This is the direct result of improper skin application at the factory. It is hard to get to because it is below the front floorboards. The correct repair would be to remove and replace the rivets by the best shop practice method. This will skin up the paint, so it is best to form a couple of stiffeners and rivet them to the offending area.

Sometimes a skin panel in the fuselage belly will buzz. This is hard to detect. The easiest way to locate the offensive panel is to remove all the floorboards and go fly the airplane. While in flight, touch a finger to each panel, between stringers and bulkheads. You can feel the panel buzz. Of course, a stiffener added to the panel will correct the problem.

Sometimes a skin panel on the flat side of the aft fuselage will can slightly. In this case install panels of Scotch Foam Y-370 made by the 3M Company. This material is very light and has a self-adhesive. It is very effective.

AIRFRAME FATIGUE

Some people ask how many hours a Bonanza airframe is good for. It's hard to tell. I know of one, years ago, that had 17,000 hours. Even though they had been hard hours, this particular airplane still looked like new.

I have worked with a fleet of Bonanzas that would accumulate 5000 hours in two years and there was no sign of fatigue. Once in a while a crack might appear in, say, a stablizer skin. Such a crack is not necessarily the result of fatigue, but is basically caused by an oil can condition, which usually is a direct result of improper rivet procedure during manufacture. If the crack is, say, one inch long, it should be stop-drilled. Once a built-in stress relieves itself by cracking, the crack will seldom progress further.

There have been cases where stabilizers on the "V" tail Bonanzas have been removed that revealed cuts in the spar web. They were caused by skin on the fuselage spar cut out, chafing the spar. In all cases, the skin edge contact had relieved itself so the chafing action had stopped. This chafing resulted from insufficient clearance for the spar attach point during manufacture. The "V" tail stabilizer spar is several times stronger than normal requirements. This is an unusual condition found in only a few airplanes, but if it is yours, it could be of concern, but should not be.

Bonanzas, like most airplanes, have water drain holes in the fuselage belly. The factory discovered that when the airplane was flown in the rain, these drain holes turned into a base for small fountains of water inside the fuselage. There have been isolated cases where this water turned to ice and froze the controls. Starting about the V35B, scuppers were added over the holes causing a negative pressure. These scuppers bond to the skin and are Part No. S43.

STRUCTURAL INTEGRITY

We don't think much about the structural integrity of an airplane until we hit tremendous clear air turbulance, or we fly into a thunderstorm or we become disoriented in the clouds and come roaring out at 300 miles an hour. Then structural integrity becomes a big factor.

I have watched the Bonanza series from the beginning and know that it had a complete wind tunnel test background. Each of its components have been tested over and over.

The Bonanza series was licensed in the utility category which means that its ultimate design load factor must be 6.6 times its gross weight. This also means that a utility category airplane is 15.7 percent stronger than one built in the normal category. The Bonanza is stressed to an 8 G ultimate load factor. The Bonanza is a well-balanced airplane structurally. This tells us that the engine compartment, the fuselage, the wings and the tail will withstand about the *same* ultimate structural loads. As in everything else the Bonanza is only as strong as its weakest link. This weakest link varies with the Model 35 series and within the Model 33 and 36 series. Other factors dictate the portion of the airplane that fails first. When the loads are applied, the airplane attitude, CG loading and airspeed all are contributing factors. But the final factor is when the structural limits have been exceeded.

In Bonanzas prior to the C35, the wing would fail first, most likely in the landing light area. In Bonanzas from the C35 thru the G35, failure might occur in the tail or wing, but a different location in the wing. Starting with the Serial D-4251 thru mid-G35, the wing spar was strengthened to carry the increased airplane weight. In these models the tail is most likely to fail first. In the Model 33 and 36 series, which are later generation models, the wing will fail first.

There are differences between the Model 35 series and the Model 33 and 36 series. Stick forces on the 35 series are generally lighter. CG limits are different. There are differences in the angle of incidence settings within the Model 35 series and between the Model 35 and 33 and 36 series stabilizers. All these factors determine when the ultimate structural limits are exceeded on a given portion of the airplane.

In the "V" tail series we see signs of flexibility in the attach points. This flexibility is desirable and in no way contributes to failure. The tail structure could be made more rigid. This would do one of two things: move the loads elsewhere, or cause the structure to break. There is a very simple solution to all this. **Do not exceed the structural limits.** If you get in trouble, slow the airplane down. Level the wings. Extend the landing gear and lift the nose with the trim tab. If you anticipate trouble, slow the airplane and extend the gear and flaps. Set a shallow descent and you won't get into trouble.

RESKINNING CONTROL SURFACES

As your Bonanza grows older and especially if you live close to the sea, you may find that areas of the control surface skins look like a piece of old lace. Control surfaces on the early Bonanzas were made with magnesium skins which, of course, had a tendency to corrode. The ailerons were changed to aluminum at airplane Serial D-6586, (N35) and aluminum flaps started at Serial D-3951, (the E35). This change resulted in a much improved service life.

Ruddervator skins are still made of magnesium. Magnesium weighs about half as much as aluminum, so in a ruddervator, it is easier to balance but harder to maintain. The use of polyurethane primers provide a giant step in the service life of magnesium skins. If you order new ruddervator skins, they will arrive primed inside and out.

If your aileron was magnesium and you decide to reskin, the new skin will be aluminum. Before applying the skin, be sure to apply two coats of primer to the rib contact area to prevent corrosion caused by the dissimilar metals. Aileron skins are interchangeable but flap skins and ruddervators are right and left. The problem in reskinning control surfaces is to get them to fit. If you don't have tooling, and most shops don't, then it is best to temporarily assemble the surface by installing clamps or cleco buttons. Hang the surface on the wing to determine correct alignment, then put it back on the bench and rivet it up.

MAGNETIC COMPASS DEVIATION

Sometimes after your Bonanza has been worked on, your magnetic compass will suddenly give erroneous readings. This is usually caused by something back of ihe instrument panel becoming magnetized. Since the control column is about the only steel in the area, it is the most logical source of trouble. You see, it takes only a hot electrical wire arcing against the steel shaft to magnetize the shaft, so it is easy to accidentally do the job. An engine crankshaft can be magnetized too, but it is less likely to occur. Both parts can be demagnetized, so it is something that can be fixed. Sometimes an electrical wire carrying high current will deflect a compass, but this will be easier to find.

BONANZA BRAKES

The early Model 35 Bonanzas used a Firestone brake and a VI-15-875 master cylinder. The Firestone brake Part No. CFA 299 was a good, but a fairly complex brake. This brake was replaced by a Part

No. 952968 Goodyear brake that was also good but a simpler brake to maintain. A master cylinder Part No. VI-15-625 was used with this brake thru the Model G35.

A still different Goodyear brake assembly gear drive with a single puck was used on the H35 Serial D-4866 thru D-7214 which was about the middle of the P35 production. Starting with Serial D-6493, (M35) thru D-7151, the same basic brake was used, except this one used two brake pucks.

Starting with Serial D-7109, the later P35 series, thru D-8501 the V35, still another Goodyear brake was used. This was a good stopping brake, but it caused drag and made the airplane hard to push. The kidney-type pucks wore unevenly so puck life was not especially good.

Starting with D-9192, the Cleveland brake was used and is still used on the Model 33 and V35B series. This is not only a good stopping brake but it is easy to maintain. The Cleveland will adapt to any of the Bonanza models. Even the Cleveland brake used on the Baron will adapt. However, the Baron brake is really more brake than is needed on a Bonanza.

The Baron brakes use a centered iron brake puck that is very hard and must be glazed by heat. To do this, you taxi at 50 MPH and severely set the brakes until they become very hot. This is hard on the brake disc, so in some cases the smaller Bonanza brake that uses organic brake pucks is better and lasts longer.

Baron rudder pedals are longer than Bonanza pedals but not much longer. If the Baron brake is used on the Bonanza, some STC approval calls for the Baron master brake cylinder to be installed. The longer master cylinder will fit, but it throws the rudder brake pedal aft at an uncomfortable angle cramping the pilot's ankles. There is not enough adjustment to compensate, so the shorter Bonanza master brake cylinder should be used.

The parking brake on the Bonanza is indirectly and directly responsible for air entering the hydraulic brake system. In Bonanzas prior to the Model S35, the parking brake valve was located between the master brake cylinder and the hydraulic fluid reservoir. With the brake check valve in this location in the system, hydraulic pressure would build as you pumped the brakes to set the parking brakes. As you pulled on the parking brake control, you trapped this pressure between the brake master cylinders and the brake on the wheel. This pressure would cause the seals on the master cylinders to leak fluid and to allow air to enter the system. The parking brake check valve also would sometime allow air to enter the system. Starting with the S35, the parking brake valve was relocated between the master brake cylinders and the wheel cylinders. This relieved the pressure on the master brake cylinders, making air in the hydraulic lines less of a problem. The master brake cylinder is installed with the piston rod on top, so any dirt from the pilot's shoes on the rudder pedal will fall on the exposed end of the master cylinder. This dirt works into the master cylinder "O" ring seal, causing it to leak fluid. Beech installed a simple chamois boot on the master cylinder piston and master cylinder body which kept the dirt out. Then some factory worker suggested the boot be removed. Now dirt can fall. You can make a boot and tie it in place with string.

There have been cases when the master brake cylinder piston rod was bent. This was not caused by applying the brakes, but was the result of overtorquing the bolt in the clevis end of the piston rod at the brake pedal or overtorquing the master brake cylinder mounting bolt. Sometimes a brake may not release even though the master brake cylinder piston rod is not bent. Then it is a sticking check valve inside the master brake cylinder. The Beech parts catalogue shows spare parts, so the part can be rebuilt.

When Cleveland brake kits are installed, the original brake hose on the strut is used. This hose is too long with the Cleveland brake, so bows outward to the extent it strikes the edge of the wheel well. It can even jam the landing gear doors. When the strut is extended, the hose should have only a slight bow.

There is another rubber hose at the front main gear shock strut hinge. Sometimes the brake line fitting is positioned so the hose must flex at the very edge of the hose fitting as the gear retracts or extends. This concentration of flex will cause the hose to fail. Changing the angle of the fitting will spread out the flex and save the hose.

REPAIR AFTER BELLY LANDING

Sometimes the best of us get careless for just an instant and suddenly find that we have bellied our pride and joy Bonanza, one that we may have flown without incident for five years or so.

The question is, what do we do to fix it up? Will it ever fly as good again? Most important, will be be as strong?

A good belly landing, if there is such a thing, does very little actual structural damage. The Bonanza belly was made flat to lessen damage when bellied in. The prop, nose gear doors, main gear doors and flaps suffer the most. If the gear retract handle was moved instead of the flap retract handle, or if you simply forgot to extend the gear on landing, the gear doors suffer very little damage. The prop and belly will sustain the most damage. Usually in this sort of landing, the lower nose bug will sustain some damage. If the nose gear doors are damaged to any great extent, the lower engine keel will be damaged. Antennas on the belly tear skin real "good."

Most shops will replace damaged keel parts and belly bulkheads. The belly bulkheads are made so that they can be easily spliced. Sometimes the low bidder will straighten the bent part. If he does a good job, it too is OK, except it is more obvious that repair has been made. If new parts are used to replace damaged parts, the new parts will have pilot holes that make it possible to align parts perfectly, eliminating the need for tooling to achieve exact alignment. In more serious accidents where the engine compartment is extensively damaged, it is best to order out a complete nose section.

The Bonanza fuselage itself is made up in four sections: the lower cabin, the upper cabin, the nose engine compartment and the aft fuselage. In cases of extensive damage, the damage can be repaired by ordering individual parts. This may be difficult to do since one part may be back ordered and could hold up the entire job from four weeks to six months. In the long run, it is better to replace the damaged section from a cost standpoint, a time standpoint and an alignment standpoint.

In cases where a wing has been severely damaged, sometimes it is cheaper to install a used wing. However, be careful. Find a wing preferably off the same model airplane or from a later model. All wings will physically fit; however, wing bolt size differs and spar strength varies considerably, so choose a replacement wing carefully.

If a wing leading edge is damaged, say, two feet in from the tip, buy a new leading edge section from Beech, so that the wing will assemble properly. You see, the wing has two degrees of twist and the twist is achieved through the wing leading edge spar section.

Of course, if damage is local, such as a bird hit, the damaged area can be cut away and a flush patch applied. If flush rivets and filler are used, the patch will hardly be noticed.

Once in a while a mechanic will install a snap ring in the top of a landing gear strut, backward. Snap rings have one rounded edge and one sharp edge. If the rounded edge is installed against pressure, the snap ring will work out of its groove, allowing the strut cap to blow upward and through the wing skin. It makes a very jagged three-inch hole in the wing. A flush patch should be used to repair the damage.

Skins can be overstressed from flight loads, from hard landings and from striking objects like runway shoulders with the landing gear. Overstressing can be detected by noting wrinkles in the skins. Hard landings will show diagonal wrinkles on the top of the wing and wrinkles in the fuselage side skins, emanating from the wing fittings. Some wrinkles can be noted just outboard of the landing gear doors. If the landing gear strikes a curb-like object, it can cause wrinkles in the rear spar web. There is a repair procedure to add vertical stiffeners to the rear spar to offset this damage. Skin wrinkles look worse than they really are. You see, it takes a like load to bend the wrinkle the second time. Of course, there are exceptions. If the spar cap is straight, the wing is most likely not hurt. In this kind of damage, rivets should be removed from only one section of damaged skin at a time. Oftentimes, the structure below the wrinkled skin will pop back into place once the damaged skin is removed. Replacing the skin will usually make it good as new.

Some spar damage repair can be accomplished, but personally, I would prefer it be replaced. Airplanes based close to the sea sometimes will corrode. Generally speaking, this corrosion is not especially detrimental to aluminum parts. There is one exception to this and that is inner granular corrosion. This is corrosion that turns a spar cap or wing stringer to a white powder and will totally destroy the structural strength of the part. In spar caps, the corrosion can be detected by a raised bump below the paint. Poke a sharp object, such as an ice pick, into the bump. If the ice pick penetrates into the spar, replace the spar.

A CASE OF TROUBLE

On climb out and cruise and IO-470 engine, a persistent roughness or miss was encountered. It wasn't a constant thing. Just every few seconds it would misfire. The fuel injection system was checked, component by component, but the miss continued. The entire fuel injection system, fuel pump, metering valve and manifold valve were replaced. The injector nozzles were cleaned. Both magnetos were checked and were good. The spark plug harness was checked and was good. The engine was rebuilt with new bearings, new rings, new valve guides. When it was run, the miss was still there. Everything was checked and everything changed *except the hydraulic valve lifters.* A partial sticking hydraulic valve lifter will produce the exact miss just described. Continental Motors has had hydraulic lifter troubles, so if all else fails, replace the lifters. In this case, it was only an occasional sticking lifter, but still it is better to replace them all.

NEXT CASE

Your IO-470 engine was enjoying fair oil consumption, one quart in six hours. Suddenly it starts to use one quart in one or two hours. There is oil on the belly. Of course there could be a broken piston ring but that is not likely. So before you spend a lot of money, install a new crankshaft seal.

When the old seal is removed, you may notice that it has worn a slight groove in the crankshaft. If so, use a strip of emery cloth and polish out the worn groove so that the new seal will seat on a flat surface. What happens here, as the crankshaft seal wears, it allows air to enter the crankcase which pressurizes the crankcase and this forces oil out the breather tube.

TROUBLE SHOOTING
TROUBLE WITH A LESSON TO BE LEARNED

Here are two cases of trouble with a lesson to be learned.

On engine shutdown, the pilot had a habit of moving the propeller by hand to a horizontal position. On this occasion the engine was frozen solid. Investigation revealed that the starter Bendix drive and clutch were welded solid and were blue from heat. A new starter was installed and the starter and engine operated in a normal manner. Five hours later, the replacement starter froze solid, showing signs of heat.

Now, let's go back to the lesson to be learned. Starters normally give good service and the Bendix drive and clutch should never show signs of heat. This should have alerted the mechanic to other troubles, but instead he just installed a new starter. The owner was alerted to look for another source of trouble. Before he could have the work done, the second $1,100 starter was shot. This time an effort was made to find the source of the trouble, which turned out to be a plugged oil passage in the engine.

The second case, the engine quit on roll out after landing. The service mechanic determined that the engine-driven fuel pump fuel pressure was below minimum limits, 7 PSI. The mechanic adjusted the fuel pressure but could raise pressure to just barely 9 PSI. It should be 9 to 11 PSI. Since minimum pressure was obtained, the mechanic released the airplane. The owner wisely decided to have the pump overhauled. Overhaul was done by a different shop. On teardown, the pump was found to be full of shreds of rubber which had come from a recently installed fuel cell. Cleaning the pump restored its pressure to required limits and the engine ran great, so the airplane was returned to service.

Here again, no effort was made to determine how pieces of rubber could reach the fuel pump where there was a 20-micron filter, a screen so fine that a human hair could not pass, located between the fuel cell and the fuel pump. At the same time, no thought was given to a second 20-micron screen located in the fuel metering valve which is downstream of the pump. This is a small capacity screen that would plug easily.

Because of the lack of follow-through, the pilot's safety was jeopardized and it was necessary to take the airplane to a third mechanic.

The moral of these two stories is: locate and fix what is causing the trouble, then go a step further and determine what caused the trouble and go still another step further to find what other trouble, if any, was caused by the part failure.

ERRATIC FUEL GAGES IN THE V35

In a Model V35, the fuel gages read normal, then suddenly quit. When you turn off battery power and the fuel gages work perfectly for a short time then quit, the trouble most likely is in a resistor in the printed circuit board that opens as it heats but when cool, completes the electrical circuit.

The "E" series and IO-470 series engines in some Beech Mentors (T-34A) use a primer solenoid to aid in cold weather starts. Sometimes the primer will leak fuel, causing the engine to idle very rich and burn more fuel. It is easy to misdiagnose this condition, blaming it on the carburetor which could be a very costly mistake.

If you live in a warm climate, it might be a good idea to take this gadget off your plane.

AIR STATIC CHECK

When running an instrument air static check, the lines should be connected to the pitot line, otherwise, air pressure will back up and stretch the diaphragm in the airspeed instrument, causing it to read low.

EXHAUST VALVES

Have you ever wondered why that sweet-running engine in your Bonanza suddenly came up with low compression on one cylinder? I'm sure you asked yourself, "Have I done something wrong?" In most cases, the answer would be "No." Usually, low compression is caused by a burned or warped exhaust valve. If low compression shows up at a relatively short time after overhaul, it is most likely the result of improper seating of the valve during overhaul. On the "E" series engines, burned valves result from leaking induction pipes that will lean the mixture to that particular cylinder. Blown exhaust gaskets can cause the valve to warp or the hot exhaust gases will cause a hot spot in the cylinder head that in turn causes heat buildup in the valve.

On fuel-injected engines, a partially plugged injector nozzle will cause a lean mixture that will burn or warp a valve.

Low unmetered fuel pump pressure can cause lean mixture at take-off power, but this would most likely cause valve trouble in more than one cylinder. When you find low compression and burned valves on one cylinder, look around the outside of the cylinder for the cause.

LIGHT OR HEAVY CRANKCASE

How can you tell if your IO-520 engine has a light or heavy case? Check Continental Service Bulletin M77-14 Rev. 1. The heavy case has a series of lumps along the top ridge.

ENGINE QUITS ON ROLL OUT

What do you look for when your engine quits on roll out? **Carburetor engines**—improper idle mixture, too-low RPM, and low fuel pressure. **Fuel-injected engines**—wear in throttle, metering linkage, throttle arm moving independently of metering arm on throttle shaft. Improper idle mixture, low fuel pressure or pressure altitude.

OIL ON REAR SEAT CARPET BY HAND CRANK

Too high oil level in landing gear gearbox.

GEAR LUBE COMES OUT VENT HOLE IN LANDING GEAR GEARBOX

Too much lube in gearbox.

AIRSPEED INDICATOR READS ERRATIC

Water in airspeed static line.

AFTER LANDING, MAIN GEAR INBOARD DOOR HANGS OPEN

Low power in landing gear motor.

PROP SPINNER FORWARD SUPPORT BRACKET OR REAR BULKHEAD CRACKS

Rear bulkhead bent, spinner attach bolt holes misaligned.

"E" SERIES ENGINE WON'T START

Idle cutoff valve in carburetor sticks open.

THROTTLE OR MIXTURE CONTROL CREEPS

Leather friction washer worn. Loosen hex nut back of intrument panel, tighten nut on front side of panel.

MAGNETIC COMPASS ERRATIC

Control column in instrument panel magnetized.

IN TURBOCHARGED ENGINE, LOW MANIFOLD PRESSURE ABOVE 7000 FT.

Dirty or improper induction air filter, sticking waste gate, leak in induction air system, coked blower.

KIT FOR HIGHER EMERGENCY LANDING GEAR ON MODEL 35 & B35 SERIES

Parts involved: Beech Kit 35-603 and 35-604.

1 ea. 35-825074-1   spring
1 ea. 002-410038-3 shaft
1 ea. 35-825191-1   rod
1 ea. 35-825191-3   rod
1 ea. 35-815003-1   rod
1 ea. 45-815003-3   rod
1 ea. 35-815007-4   link

EXCESSIVE UNEVEN MAIN GEAR TIRE WEAR

If the main gear tire wears uneven on one shock strut, and the airplane is hard to push, try switching the strut torque knees from one strut to the other. If this doesn't correct the problem, the strut may have been misaligned during manufacture, so contact the factory.

ERRATIC FUEL GAGES IN V35 SERIES

Most likely trouble source, printed circuit boards located above fuel gage on back side of instrument panel. Check first for overtorqued PC board attach screws. Switch sides of PC board control. Don't overtorque PC board attach screws.

FUEL SIPHONS FROM FUEL TANK THROUGH VENT TUBE

Check for sticking fuel siphon. Check valve. Check valve outboard of fuel tank. (Access panel on bottom side of wing.) Check valve vent tube (on bottom side of wing) for obstructions that plug the tube.

BOTTOM OF FUEL TANK LIFTS AS FUEL BURNS OFF

Improperly positioned fuel vent tube, should extend 1-3/4 inches and be bent forward 10 degrees and chamfered at 45 degrees; or vent is plugged.

WHERE DO YOU LEAN IO-470 AND IO-520 ENGINES?

In cruise 50 degrees below EGT peak.

CLEANING OIL COOLER TANK AND RADIATOR ON "E" SERIES ENGINES

Any time metal is detected in the engine or when oil cooling problems occur, the oil cooler assembly should be cleaned. Flush the tank with kerosene or distillate and then submerge the cooler in a tank filled with kerosene or distillate and allow it to soak four hours. After soaking, again flush thoroughly with clean kerosene or distillate.

THINGS TO WATCH FOR IN THE EMERGENCY
LANDING GEAR RETRACT SYSTEM

Never retract the landing gear with the emergency hand crank. It can damage the worm gear drive. Always pull the landing gear circuit breaker before engaging and moving the hand crank. Keep the floorboard area below the hand crank clear of debris or too-thick carpet. After the gearbox has been worked on, try out the hand crank for rotation. The crank can be installed wrong. On the V35B, 36A and F33A series, be sure the emergency hand crank will extend from the retract position after each 100-hour inspection or any time the spar cover has been removed. If improperly installed, the spar cover will cover the emergency hand crank cover, making it impossible to engage the hand crank.

FUEL BOOST PUMPS

On fuel-injected engines, use the fuel boost pump to prime the engine only. Then turn the boost pump off. When the engine-driven pump is pumping and the boost pump is on high, fuel mixture will be too rich.

NON-CONGEALING OIL RADIATORS ARE NOT APPROVED
FOR THE IO-470 SERIES ENGINE

You can position a strip of three-inch duct tape across the center face of the cooler to prevent oil congealing. Make that three thicknesses of tape.

UNEVEN FUEL FLOW FROM AUXILIARY FUEL TANKS
IN F35 THRU H35 BONANZAS

This is caused by a check valve in the fuel line coming from the auxiliary tank that doesn't feed down. The check valve is in the wheel well. Take the check valve apart and free up the flapper valve spring. Install the check valve with the embossed arrow pointing inboard and the word "hinge" on the top side.

AFTER A PROP STRIKE

Have the engine torn down and the crankshaft magnifluxed. You may have to argue with your insurance company, but they don't fly your airplane.

WHEN THE VOLTAGE REGULATOR QUITS ON YOUR EARLY SERIES BONANZA

The regulator is Part No. 118713 which is no longer available. Order Part No. 1119224. This number supercedes the old number and is still available. Cost of the voltage regulator is rather high, so try locating a used one at an aircraft salvage yard.

OIL DRIPS FROM ENGINE INDUCTION PIPE DRAIN

Black oil residue leaks out of fuel manifold drain lines and drips on the floor. This oil may appear five minutes after engine shutdown. This condition can occur on normally aspirated or turbocharged engines. The source of the oil is oil seeping through the engine valve guides. This occurs after landing and as you taxi. It will also occur as you run turbocharged engines at low RPM to cool down turbochargers. This is not necessarily an indication of worn valve guides, but it could be. Some valve guides contain what would amount to mill marks in a swirl pattern. These marks are designed to return oil in the guides to the crankcase. It is fairly easy to pinpoint which cylinders are at fault on the IO-470 or IO-520 series engines. Each cylinder induction pipe is connected to the adjacent cylinder induction pipe with a rubber hose. It is about three inches long and is held in position with two clamps.

To check an individual cylinder, slip the hose back so that you can see up inside each cylinder's induction pipe. If the pipe is free of oil, then go to the next cylinder. Since oil is sucked past the valve guide only at low power, as when taxiing, it is not going to add to oil consumption to any marked degree. Other than causing a mess on the floor, it is not going to hurt anything. Continental Motors has a kit available that installs felt sleeves over the valve guides. This kit will solve the problem and can be installed without removing the cylinder. It is covered in Continental Motors Service Letter M76-24TS, Revision 1, Supplement 1.

CABIN EXHAUST VENT

The side cabin exhaust vent is great. It helps air to flow through the cabin, but it is noisy. Insert a bracket sponge induction air filter in the exhaust vent hose to quiet the ever-present air noise. While it will quiet the noise, it won't restrict airflow.

OIL TEMP BULB ON "E" SERIES ENGINES

On "E" Series engines, too long an oil temp bulb will hold the oil check valve open, allowing oil to drain into the engine sump from the oil tank.

IMPROPER MAGNETO TIMING

This can cause detonation which can burn holes in pistons. Most magnetos lay relatively flat on the engine. If they mount in, say, a 45 degree position, internal timing is off.

COMPASS DEFLECTION

Something is causing the compass to deflect. The most common source of trouble is a magnetized control column. If a "hot" wire comes in contact with the steel control column causing an arc, the column will magnetize. Fortunately, the column can be demagnetized. A lightning strike can magnetize the engine crankshaft. This can be detected by removing the propeller and checking the shaft with a meter. If the crankshaft is magnetized, the engine must be disassembled to demagnetize it. Electrical circuits below the glareshield can also cause compass deflection. There is no need to replace the compass because once the magnetic deflection has been removed, the compass will read normally.

VIBRATION

You have an S35 or later Bonanza with three-blade propeller. You also have wing tip tanks and vibration in the airframe. Add aileron gap strips to the lower wing skins, just forward of the aileron. The tip tanks don't cause the vibration. It is the three-blade propeller frequency that causes the vibration. Changing to a two-blade prop will get rid of the bulk of the vibration, but gap strips are easier to install.

GENERATOR BELTS

As a rule, generator belts give good service life and require little attention. If a belt does break or jump off the pulley, we normally check for belt quality or pulley alignment as the cause of the trouble. Sometimes we run into belt trouble after an engine overhaul. It is very frustrating to encounter belt troubles when the pulleys align, the belt tension is correct and the belt is of high quality. In this case, we have a hidden source of trouble.

In all flat engines, such as the Lycoming and Continental, the crankshaft twists back and forth along its length, winding and unwinding very slightly at a rate of something like 200 times per second. This makes the crankshaft's rotation somewhat jerky. Left uncorrected, it can cause the generator belt to flop up and down violently, causing the belt to fail. This same crankshaft twist condition can feed stress into propeller blades which can cause propeller blades to fail.

To cure this condition, install the correct combination of index pins in the crankshaft counterweights. Crankshaft counterweights are secured to the crankshaft with pins. How tight the pins fit is determined by order such as fifth or sixth order pin. The sixth order pin is a tighter fit than a fifth order pin. It's not a big job to change these pins but the cylinder on one bank must be removed to gain access to the counterweights. Work with the engine manufacturer to determine where each pin goes.

VALVE LIFTERS

Look for flat valve lifters when you start the engine up cold and it runs rough, then after 30 to 60 seconds, it smooths out.

Sometimes on climb out the engine runs rough. If magnetos, plugs and ignition harness check OK, look for flat valve lifters.

OIL LEAKS

There is a new oil leak below the forward end of the IO-520 Series engine. Oil looks clean and fresh but it is in quantity. There is a small plate about an inch-and-a-quarter long that covers the end of the camshaft that is sealed with a gasket. It is held in position on the front crankcase by two bolts located below the crankshaft. It is hard to see. Remove the access plate over the prop governor and remove the landing light in the nose bug to gain access. Reseal, if necessary. Most likely, all that is needed is to tighten the bolts to stop the leaks.

PROP SPINNERS

If a prop spinner runs true and its support brackets and bulkheads run true, the spinner should run forever. Sometimes the rear bulkhead on the Beech 215 electric prop and the Beech 278 prop will crack and the front support bracket or attach bolt will break. This part failure is the direct result of damage inflicted when the prop was removed. If the spinner is cracking or the front support bracket or bolt is breaking, remove the spinner, start and idle the engine, then stand off to the side of the propeller in line with the rear bulkhead. Eyeball the bulkhead as it turns. If it doesn't run true, it will cause the spinner and support hardware to break. What causes the rear bulkhead to wobble? Most generally, it results when the prop is removed and laid down on the rear bulkhead. The weight of the prop bends the bulkhead.

CHROME PLATED SPINNERS

A chrome-plated spinner is a sight to behold. While it is beautiful, it is not always satisfactory. You see, the aluminum spinner must be plated with copper before it can be chrome plated. This is difficult to do and the copper doesn't always hold. Consequently, the chrome comes off, which makes it unsatisfactory. There are several shops that chrome spinners.

SPINNER REPAIR

Spinners are made by a spinning process that stretches metal over a wood block. The metal used is soft aluminum, so while it is most difficult to straighten a bent spinner, a cracked spinner can be welded by a competent welder.

"SHOWER OF SPARKS" & MAGNETOS

When a "shower of sparks" was first introduced on the Bonanza, it was heralded as something new. The "shower of sparks" idea has been around a long time. In fact, the Model T Ford and Pierce Arrow used shower of sparks. The "shower of sparks" coil produces a shower of sparks that is wired into a set of points in a magneto. This set of points provides retarded timing and is used for starting. Once the engine starts, a second advanced set of points takes over. Once the starter switch is relaxed, the "shower of sparks" stops.

The impulse coupling, in most cases, is more reliable, but it, too, has had its problems, mainly from lack of maintenance. The latest bulletin deals with improper material used by Bendix in the manufacture of the coupling.

There was a period of time that Continental Motors installed Slick magnetos. This is a good magneto but it, too, had its problems. The cam or follower block would wear, so point gap would decrease. This resulted in more frequent maintenance. The Slick factory is easy to work with and took prompt care of any trouble they might have. The Bendix magneto is generally recognized as a more reliable magneto, but like Slick, they, too, have had their problems.

In overhauling magnetos, mechanics sometimes get internal timing off. This can be detected by the way the magneto is mounted on the engine. If it mounts at an odd angle, the magneto will work in this condition but not as efficiently as if it were timed right.

MOUNTING AILERONS

There is little need to remove ailerons, except for painting. Sometimes when they are removed and reinstalled, the mechanic misses the bolt mounting hole in the hinge. This results in the aileron being attached by one hinge. It is easy to spot this condition. Look at the gap between the wing trailing edge and the aileron. If the gap is wider at one end, the aileron is mounted wrong. I have found this condition several times in the Service Clinics.

PROPELLER AND ENGINE RPM RESTRICTIONS

You may read in your owner's manual to use, say, 2650 RPM for take off for one minute and 2300 RPM for all other operations. You may have installed a Hartzell propeller who's limit is, say, 2700 RPM, so the questions is, what RPM can you use for take off, climb and cruise?

The reason for the 2650 RPM limitation for one minute is stress being fed into the prop blades by the combination of engine crankshaft and crankshaft counterweight. This feeds dangerous stress into the prop blades and could lead to blade failure.

How about the Hartzell prop limit of RPM? This simply means that the prop will not throw a blade at 2700 RPM or below. This has nothing to do with a blade breaking at a lower RPM, caused by stress imposed on the blade by the crankshaft and counterweight combination.

SHORTENING PROP BLADES

When a factory such as Beech develops a propeller blade length, they start out with a blade length that is longer than they plan to use. They cement strain gages to the blade and run the prop engine combination at the most desirable RPM. They measure blade stress. They shorten the blade by one-half inch, then measure the stress again. This shortening of the blade and measuring stress continues until the stress reading bottoms out and starts to climb as the blade is shortened further. So a length is established that gives the least stress for a given RPM. This is why you must be careful about changing props.

ROCK NICKS IN PROP BLADES

A rock nick can set up a stress point in a propeller blade that can lead to a crack and eventual blade failure. A deep rock nick in the blade's leading edge six inches from the tip is especially dangerous. The sharp crevice created by the rock should be radiused out with a fine rat-tail file and the filed area smoothed by fine emery cloth, followed by crocus cloth.

Rock nicks on the back side of the blade are prime spots for cracks. This type of a gouge should be burnished out with a burnishing tool. You notice, I recommend smoothing beyond filing. Files leave sharp crevices that, in themselves, can create stress points.

AIR LEAKS IN THE CABIN

When you hear air leaks around the cabin windows and door, it is air leaking from inside the cabin outboard through improperly seated seals. Air pressure within the cabin, forces the seals outboard around the windows and doors, sealing out the air noise.

The rubber cabin door seal basically keeps out rain. The round windlace that is secured to the door opening in the fuselage seals out air leaks. As you fly and detect air leaks around the cabin door, press on the round windlace. If you find that you can stop the air noise by pushing on a given area of the windlace, mark the area. When you are on the ground, loosen the flush machine screws that position the windlace to the fuselage. Once the machine screws are removed from the area of the marked air leak, slip the windlace **outboard** to give the windlace more flexibility. This allows air pressure inside the cabin to push the windlace against the cabin door, closing the leak.

Often times new window seals are installed unnecessarily. To check for air leaks around the rear windows, open the window. Insert a one inch wide strip of paper over the window seal and close the window. If you can pull the paper free, you have found the air leak area. Start at the top of the window and work around the window perimeter. It is easy to seal this kind of leak. The rubber window seal is cemented to a sheet metal lip that is about .025 inch thick. To stop the air leak, simply tap on the metal lip hard enough to spring the lip outboard a few thousandths of an inch and you have stopped the air leak. In most cases a new seal is not needed.

HIGH OIL CONSUMPTION

Sometimes, for no reason at all, you might find the airplane belly coated with oil. Usually, this discovery is followed by an increase in oil consumption. There are several possible causes, a broken piston ring, an excessively worn valve guide or a blown seal at the front crankshaft seal. This seal will allow air to enter the crankcase which forces oil out the breather line. Sometimes the seal will wear a shallow groove in the crankshaft. This groove must be burnished out before a new seal will seal.

SERVICE CLINIC DISCREPENCIES AND THEIR FIX

Fuel siphons from tanks

There is a siphon break valve just outboard of the fuel tank. It can be reached through an access panel on the underneath side of the wing. Check the siphon break valve vent tube which is in some cases flush with the wing or it may protrude 1/16 to 1/8 inch. Be sure this hole is open. If the vent line is open, remove the siphon break check valve. The hex nut unscrews, revealing a spring loaded check valve. Free up the flapper valve and re-install the valve. Position the embossed arrow pointing inboard and the word "hinge" on the top side of the valve.

Cowl flap control linkage out of rig

Cowl flaps should work easily and once closed should remain closed. Cowl flaps are controlled by a flexible control that comes through the right-hand side of the firewall. This control connects to an "L" shaped arm that is bolted to a cross shaft that crosses the nose compartment keel. When closed, the control rod that connects the "L" shaped control arm to the cowl flap should be positioned so as to just cross the center of the forward edge of the cross shaft hole. In this position, the cowl door controls form a cam lock which prevents the doors from moving in flight.

Cleveland brakes

Cleveland brakes seldom give trouble. We have found the disc mounting flange cracked at the wheel. Brake discs rust badly near salt water and there is nothing that can be done to clear up rust. Cleveland discs can be chrome plated but only if organic lining is used. The Baron brake uses a centered iron lining that is extremely hard. This lining will tear up chrome plating.

Some Bonanzas were equipped with Goodyear multi-disc brakes. This is a fine brake that gives very little trouble. Like all brakes, they will wear out and replacement parts are costly. When it is time to buy new discs, it uses three per wheel, weigh the cost of replacement against the cost of new Cleveland brakes.

WHAT TO DO

BUYING ANOTHER ENGINE

It's time to buy a rebuilt or remanufactured engine. What kind of cylinders should I get? If you live close to the sea or in an area of high humidity, select chrome cylinders. Generally speaking, steel cylinders will have built-in choke and they break-in faster. They will rust if not used regularly. Continental Motors are not using chrome cylinders on their remanufactured engines.

WORN TIRES

Your main gear tires are worn. Should I buy a new tire or a retread? Buy a new tire. As tires wear, the tire body increases in size, so when new tread is added the overall tire diameter is larger and it may not clear the wheel well.

THE HANGAR DOOR BLEW IN ON MY BONANZA

The hangar door blew in on my Bonanza and mashed the cabin in. Should I rebuild by buying individual parts or an assembly? Buy the assembly. The fuselage itself is built in four major pieces. The engine compartment, the lower cabin floor, the upper cabin and the aft fuselage. If you can find a used part in salvage, it will fit. New sections would be best but lead time is unreal. A used part will get you back in the air sooner. Beech tooling is excellent, so alignment is no problem.

VERTICAL SCALE INSTRUMENTS

Beech installed vertical scale instruments in a number of Bonanzas. They were not very satisfactory, so most were replaced under warranty. There were a few that didn't get changed. Now there are no replacements. The Aero Mock Company in Wichita can rebuild the instruments. Tex Sun in Amarillo has a few new instruments in stock at this writing.

TAKING PICTURES FROM A BONANZA

If you want to take super pictures from a Bonanza, try the Model 36 and remove the back doors. It is best to add a small wind deflector on the front door post and tie a rope around your waist. Your insurance won't be much good, so be careful. The Bonanza can be flown with the passenger window removed for picture taking, just don't make a habit of it.

MUFFLERS

Inside both mufflers there are perforated cones called flame cones. These cones are welded to the muffler body and are part of the muffler. The cones quiet exhaust noise. In the case of the heater muffler, the cone directs hot exhaust gas against the heater shell to make the heater more effective. The continuous heat and exhaust pressure can cause the cone to erode, crack and break loose from the muffler shell.

If the cone breaks loose in one piece it can jam in the exhaust opening and cause severe engine back pressure and loss of power. Many times the cone breaks into small pieces that fall out the exhaust pipe. This process will continue until the cone is completely gone. The engine can run forever with the cones out but the mufflers were certified with the cones in them. To operate without cones in is, in effect, to fly an uncertified airplane. In event of an accident and insurance claim, it could cause cancellation of your insurance. New cones can be installed reasonably. American Bonanza Society headquarters can tell you where to get them fixed.

WHAT HAPPENS WHEN CABIN DOOR POPS OPEN

If it hasn't happened to you it probably will. The cabin door pops open in flight or, most likely, on take off.

The top door latch is a cam lock and if the latch is not moved past the cam, air loads will open the cabin door. The worst part about this is the sudden loud noise. It is said that when this occurs, the pilot must get his passenger off his lap. Actually the door will fly steady in about a two-inch open position. It is extremely difficult to open the door further and it has no adverse affect on elevator or rudder control.

If it happens on the runway and you have enough runway to stop, do so, and latch the door. If you are in the air, simply go around and land. Don't try to close the door on take off run—you can get into serious trouble. The door can be latched in flight. Slow the airplane, and if your storm window opens in, open the window, slip the airplane and slam the door closed.

COWL DOOR POPS OPEN

Once in a while a cowl door will pop open in flight, especially if you have one of the new single latch controls. Don't panic, the door will fly in a partially open position and won't come off. Just land and close the door.

MEDALLIONS ON COWL DOORS

We like to pretty up our Bonanzas by installing the Beech Medallion on the cowl doors. These plates will stiffen the skin area and often-times will start a crack, so leave them off.

ODDS AND ENDS

OIL FILTER

When you want to install a full flow oil filter on your IO-470 series engine, buy Cessna kit AK-210-61L, but don't buy the filter itself. You can buy the filter separately and save money.

CONVERTING FROM THE BEECH ELECTRIC PROPELLER

When converting from the Beech electric propeller to a Hartzell propeller, you may find you cannot control propeller pitch. This is caused by oil starvation to the governor. The governor gets its oil supply from the engine driven oil pump. In some cases, the oil supply hole in the pump must be enlarged in order to supply enough oil to the propeller governor.

CHECK CLEVELAND BRAKE MOUNTING FLANGE FOR CRACKS

Brake discs sometimes will crack in the radius where the disc back plate and disc flange meet. Look for cracks around the disc attach bolt holes.

WHEN YOU INSTALL CLEVELAND BRAKES

Install shorter brake hydraulic hose. The hose used on the old Goodyear brakes is too long for the Cleveland installation. With the strut extended, the hose should have only a gentle bend.

WATER WILL ACCUMULATE IN HYDRAULIC BRAKE LINES

Water will settle in the aluminum brake calipers at the brake disc. This accumulated water causes corrosion inside the brake caliper. Draining out a small amount of brake fluid from the brake casting at the wheel will lessen the corrosion problem.

FLEX HOSE

The flex hose between the induction air adapter and the engine induction air pipe will flex and fall apart to the extent that holes will appear. This allows unfiltered air into the engine, so check the hose for condition.

RIGHT FUEL TANK HAS A LEAK

You go out to the airport to fly your Bonanza back home and find your right fuel tank has sprung a leak and you have lost 40 gallons of fuel. You must get back home so you cannot wait several days for a new fuel tank. It is against FAA rules to take off with one empty tank. What if something happened to the other tank? What will happen if you ignore my advice and the FAA rules? Well, surprisingly enough, your airplane will fly with a full tank in only one wing, and you will have adequate aileron control to keep the wings level. Just don't make a habit of doing it.

THE FUEL DELIVERY LINES

The fuel delivery lines coming from the manifold valves to the fuel nozzles are supported by a metal bracket. The fuel lines are attached to the support brackets and are cradled in rubber. As time goes by, this rubber will shift allowing metal to metal contact between the fuel lines and the support bracket. The fuel lines can be hand formed to clear the bracket.

V35A & V35B LANDING LIGHTS

If landing gear position lights won't come on and then after you lower the flaps the landing position lights do come on, check for loose connections at the tie over bus which is located back of the circuit breaker panel. Also check the printed circuit board inside the electrical equipment junction box. Both flap and landing gear circuits are in this box.

ENGINE-DRIVEN FUEL PUMPS

Engine-driven fuel pumps on IO-470 and IO-520 engines rarely give trouble and as a rule they will talk to you of impending trouble, if you only listen. A drop or change in fuel pressure is a sign of pending trouble. There are drain lines coming from the pump, so if oil or fuel drains out of these lines, it tells you to have the pump looked at.

There are two seals inside the pump. The lower seal, seals out oil from the engine. There is a plate and a second seal that seals the fuel. We know of one case where both seals failed which allowed fuel to flow into the engine crankcase. This is a very dangerous explosive situation. You may get a bang out of it. If you see oil or fuel draining from the fuel pump, don't put off having it fixed.

PROPELLER OVERHAUL

Normally propeller overhaul is done at the same time as the engine is overhauled, but this in not necessarily so. Recently, engine TBO on the IO-520 engine was extended from 1500 to 1700 hours.

Propeller TBO was not extended, so keep this in mind when your propeller has run 1500 hours. The propeller companies are aware of this and may extend TBO, but as of this writing, it has not been done.

OIL TANK

In the model C35 thru G35 the oil tank radiator assembly has a solid rod extending from the oil line into the oil tank. This is a magnesium rod that is designed to collect corrosion. Some owners are installing quick drains on the oil drain line in the engine sump. This is good, but don't install a stiff hose on the quick drain because, if the hose extends into the nose gear wheel well, the strut might open the snap drain when the landing gear is retracted.

"E" SERIES ENGINE CYLINDERS

"E" series engine cylinders are getting a little hard to find, particularly the 538348 cylinder with the 536727 head. In addition, the price has gone up. There is a solution to this problem and that is to install the 0-470 or the I0-470 cylinders. This will require some modification of the intake exhaust system. The better cooling, longer wear and increased reliability will justify the additional expense.

VOLTAGE REGULATORS FOR GENERATORS

The voltage regulator used in Bonanzas that used generators was Part No. 1118713. This regulator is no longer available and the Beech Factory is out of stock. You can buy a superceded regulator Part No. 1119224 from an automotive parts company. It will do the job. The Part No. for the over voltage relay that works in the system is 35-3013S.

V35 FUEL GAGES

If you have a model V35 or later and the fuel gages quit after being on for a short while but when you turn off power to the gages, then turn the power back on and the gages read correctly for a short period then quit, the trouble is most likely in the resistor in the printed circuit board. When cold the resistor completes the circuit but as it heats, it breaks the circuit, then as it cools it closes the circuit. If this happens to you replace the printed circuit board.

CONTROLS CREEP IN FLIGHT

When the throttle, mixture or propeller control creeps in flight, don't buy a new control. Just loosen the retaining nut on the back side of the instrument panel and tighten the knurled nut on the front side. This tightens a leather washer that increases friction on the control.

If the throttle, mixture or propeller control bind for lack of internal lubricant, clamp a ten-inch rubber hose over the bottom end of the control. Fill the hose with light oil, install a tire valve stem on the other end of the hose and apply air pressure. This will force oil up the control.

CLEVELAND BRAKES

When new pucks are installed in Cleveland brakes and the wheels drag, check to see if the heat spacers were installed.

AIRPLANE TRIM

Your Bonanza should fly hands-off in cruise configuration. If the ball in the turn and bank, rides to one side, first level the airplane on the ground. The ball should be centered. Next check the ailerons. They should be even with the outboard end of the flap. Check the control wheel. It should be level. If it takes left rudder to center the ball, raise the left trim tab trailing edge. To do this, adjust the cables that control tab travel. Access is through the left access panel below the left stabilizer. Tighten clevis on tab cable that raises the tab, tighten one turn. Loosen the turnbuckle one turn, on the cable that lowers the tab. Fly the airplane—more or less adjustment may be needed. If the airplane flies wing heavy, try lowering the flap on the heavy wing. Don't lower it much. The right way to correct a heavy wing is to rotate the wing.

Watch out for the mechanic who dinks this and dinks that. He is guessing on rig. He can really louse things up. The right way to rig a Bonanza is to install rig tools in the tail, install rig tools in the rudder pedals, block back the elevator control and level the control wheel.

Everything on your Bonanza worked like a dream when it was new and it will do it again if it is adjusted properly and is properly lubricated.

AILERON TRIMMER

The aileron trimmer which first appeared on the model E35 is a handy gadget that is attached to the end of the control column. It was invented and built by Aircraftsman, a Beech dealer in Oklahoma City. This well-built unit seldom gives trouble, but like all mechanical things, an internal spring can break or its clutch can slip. It is hard to detect but the body is made in two pieces which unscrew to provide access to the mounting screws. The threads, in the body, are left-hand threads which get very tight if you try to unscrew them counterclockwise.

FUSELAGE COVERS

Airplanes that sit out in the weather need some kind of protection. Well-fitting covers that cover the the top of the fuselage, windshields and side windows are desirable. However, they have drawbacks. Covers made of vinyl material often contain chemicals that can cause plexiglas to craze. So be careful when selecting cover material. Fabric type material should have a soft surface to protect the glass. The cover should fit snugly to prevent dust from working up below the cover. Dust is an abrasive and will scratch the glass.

Covers that fit inside the cabin are more desirable because they protect the instruments and upholstery without the risk of scratch damage to the windshield and side windows.

EARLY TURBO-CHARGED BONANZA

Someone asked why did Beech stop building the Turbo-charged Bonanza and then years later start building it again?

It was a matter of economics. They just were not selling. When the turbo-charged engine was first introduced, it cost as much to maintain the turbo-charger as it did the airplane. The turbo-charger gave trouble. Here was a unit that ran at 1600° F at something like 27,000 RPM. The case cracked and valves stuck. The problems were worked out and today these same airplanes are relatively trouble free. Demand for turbo-charged airplanes returned, so Beech started up production, but this time in the model 36 airframe. It costs more to maintain a turbo-charged airplane but mainly at TBO time, simply because there is more to overhaul.

NOTES FROM MY LITTLE BLACK BOOK

GENERAL INFORMATION
Scuppers for fuselage belly drains: part number S43.
Air conditioner wicks: part number 490.
Landing gear gear-box lube: Mobil 636.
Elevator push rod Bulletin: number 0989.
Stick-on sound deadener: 3M product Y37D.
Belly sound deadener: Vaporite 500, Anderson Prichard Oil Co.

INSTRUMENTS
New type instrument air induction filter and parts
Covered in the Beech Service Instruction 0581-194.
Filter assembly: 1J2-1.
Washer: 960TD-1716.
Replacement filter: D9-14-15

ADHESIVES
Window sealer
Prestite 576
Pre-seal 711
Bonding agent elevator skin
EC 2216A & 2216B: (Mix 7:5 ratio, 7 parts A to 5 parts B)
Sealer prop boots
EC-801
Belly sound deadener
Vaporite 550 by Anderson Prichard Oil Co.

AIR CONDITIONERS
Relief plug set to blow at 450 PSI. Should reseal at 400 PSI. Normal pressure is around 175 PSI. Air needs to flow around condenser to prevent pressure build up.
Air conditioner STC for model 36
Parker Hannifan Corp.
Airborne Division
P.O. Box 800
Longmont, Colorado 80501
Air conditioner on IO-470
Aero Engineering Corp.
1094 Ford St.
Colorado Springs, Colorado

Tactair service information
Avionics, Inc.
Terminal Bldg.
Cincinnati, Ohio 45226

Instrument air
To adjust instrument air on Bonanza and Baron see Beech Service Instruction 012-80-Rev.-1, F33, G33, V35B and A36. If vent tube extends into wheel well, it can cause fluctuation of air pressure in instrument system if vent line contacts tire.

New instrument air filter cartrige
Part number D-9-14-5

New aluminum pump
Part number 242CW

Paper intake filter
Part number 1J-4-7

COWLING
Cowl door back-up strip: see Service Instruction 0439-242

CABIN DOOR
Inside door handle supercedes early handle: part number 95-380010
Shaft: part number 35-40464-4
Door hinge pins held in place by sheet metal screws. Remove clips and remove pins. Get to top pins through glove compartment.

ELECTRICAL
Instrument light in S35 and after
It is controlled by diodes below pilots seats, outboard diodes control avionics. Next diodes inboard control glareshield. Next inboard flight instrument lights and next inboard flight sub panel lights. Checking inverter and each panel individually is the way to isolate bad panel.

Alternator excitement
Batteries for emergency use only are located inside PC board which is inside pedestal, below throttle control. It is controlled by a relay in the alternator field circuit.

Standby generator
It works the turn co-ordinator, engine instruments, fuel quantity gage, one radio amplifier and the transponder.

"Alternator Out" sensor shunt resistor
When there is normal diode leakage in the alternator, it may prevent the "Alternator Out" sensor from turning on the "Alternator Out" light when the alternator is "off" and the battery is "on". A shunt resistor (RC20GF-202J or K) can be added to eliminate this condition.

Dim instrument lights
Add a 3500 ohm rheostat: part number XR6903.

V35 Alternator Out Light erratic
Wire size is marginal. Service Instruction 0945 shows heavier wire size.

Aircraft electrical wire
Mil-22759/16 plus gage.

Landing gear position lights
When landing gear position lights are too dim, push bulbs in toward the panel.

ENGINE

Oil temperature bulb
MS28034-1 oil temperature bulb used on IO-470C will work on IO-470G.

Engine mounts
Robbin-Tech rubber engine mounts have square sides. Lord mounts have rounded sides and should be used with three bladed propellers.

Oil leakage from induction manifold
on IO-470 and IO-520 series engines
This is caused by running the engine in low power during taxi. This can be cured by installing Continental Motor valve guide kit covered in Continental Service Letter M76TS Rev. 1, Sup.1.

EGT
Best lean: 25 degrees below peak.
Best power: 50 degrees below peak.
Smoothest power: 75 degrees below peak.

IO-520 cylinderhead temperature
It should run 380 to 400 degrees.

IO-470 oil pressure
80 PSI maximum
30 to 60 cruise
0 to 10 at idle
Oil pressure taken after circulation between number 2 and 4 cylinders.

Loss of oil pressure in the IO-470 series
It is caused by a pin the relief valve slides on. The pin length is 2.52 inches. It is covered in the Continental Bulletin M-792.

Fuel pressure gage
When the fuel pressure gage reads high but consumption is OK when pressure is taken off the manifold valve, look for rich idle mixture, plugged nozzle or high unmetered fuel pump pressure.

Throttle metering arm spring
Continental Motors part number 628-371.

High oil temperature in "E" series engine
It is caused by the oil scavenger pump. Pump should be high capacity. Impeller cavity should measure .940 and the gear should have eight teeth. See Continental Bulletin 53-2.

Changing oil temperature reading in the IO-470 series
Change the gasket thickness under the vernitherm valve. A thinner gasket to decrease temperature, thicker to increase. This changes the distance the valve has to move so cools the oil either sooner or later.

Pickling an engine for storage
See Continental Bulletin M-81-3, Rev.-1.

Thompson fuel pump kit
Part number 207910.
Check pin wear every 300 hours.

Freshly overhauled engine
Check the tachometer and manifold pressure for accuracy before starting engine.

Altimeter and manifold pressure
They should read the same atmospheric pressure. Engine will run $1\frac{1}{2}$ to 2 inches lower than field atmospheric pressure.

FUEL
Fuel transmitter resistance
Inboard 76 Ohm.
Outboard 43 ohm.

How to hook-up Rochester fuel gages
Post No. 1 connects to post No. 1 (cad) on gage. Post No. 2 center transmitter to No. 2 on instrument (brass). Post No. 3 transmitter to post No. 4 (single) outboard post case to ground.

Hand wobble pump "O" rings, C35 and after
Part number AN6227-B-15, 2 each.
Part number AN6227-B-8, 2 each.
Part number AN6227-B-7, 1 each.

Fuel printed circuit
It is covered by Service Instruction 1196, Kit 55-3023-3-S.

Fuel transmitter kit
It converts AC to Rochester Kit 55-9018-1. No gage change is required.

Fuel cap "O" ring
Part number MS29513-232.

Adel 20653 fuel boost pump
It is listed as optional equipment on G35, so no FAA form 337 is needed to install it.

SERVICE CLINIC INSPECTION

If you have ever run your Bonanza through one of the American Bonanza Society Clinics, you know that I write down any discrepancies found and personally review each item and tell you how it should be fixed. This list is only the tip of the iceberg since I look at a lot more than I write down.

Here is what I actually look at:

Propeller spinner for cracks and security.

Rear propeller spinner.

Support bulkhead for cracks.

Balance bolts in Beech Model 278 spinner (these bolts are for fine balance) and blade security in Beech propeller.

Blades should have a small amount, fore and aft movement at the tip.

Look for grease leakage at blade hub juncture caused by overgreasing.

Propeller blade for damage, especially on leading edge and on back face.

Look for cracks across face of blade.

Look closely at previous repair of rock damage, especially if file marks appear, they should be polished out with crocus cloth. Even a file mark will cause a stress concentration which can start a crack.

Look for loose prop attach bolts or signs of oil coming from prop hub that would indicate a crack.

Check exposed area of crankshaft between prop and engine and for signs of oil leaks that result from crack in crankcase.

Check front crankshaft seals for signs of leakage.

Look at engine induction air filter for condition.

The engine compartment nose bugs for cracks in area back of prop spinner and suggest stiffening area with fiberglass if needed.

Check induction air grill in nose bug for cracks and security.

Landing and taxi light for condition and security of mount.

On the IO-520 series engine, check upper crankcase for cracks, especially in the area of #1 and #3 cylinders but the crankcase in general.

Note position of magnetos that would indicate improper internal timing.

Look for drops of oil on bottom of magnetos that would indicate a magneto seal leak.

Note the crankcase type, light, modified or heavy.

Check condition of fuel manifold valve on top center of crankcase. Check vent hole.

Look for fuel stains that would reveal ruptured rubber diaphram. Check fuel lines from manifold valve to fuel nozzles.

Look for cracks and check fuel delivery lines at their support bracket. They mount in rubber but rubber slips and lines contact edge of support bracket and chafe.

Look for fuel stains in fuel delivery line attach fittings at manifold valve.

Check for position of vent hole in manifold valve. It should be on the side or in back, never on the front side.

Look at fuel nozzles. If fuel stains are prominent around base of nozzle, talk to pilot about overpriming and hot start problems.

Check ignition harness for security and obvious condition.

Look for oil leaks at the crankcase thru-bolts.

Check the rear engine baffle for cracks and especially the brace that attaches to the rear cylinder.

On models that use dry instrument air pumps, note the induction air filter.

If it is the Styrofoam garter type, suggest it be replaced by the new pleated filter.

Check the instrument air pump base.

The oil filter for oil leaks.

The bottom aft end of the starter case for a drop of oil, that would indicate starter seal leak.

Ask when the in-line instrument filter was replaced, it should be replaced every 250 hrs.

Physically, check the starter security to the crankcase.

Tighten the tachometer drive cable nut at the adapter drive.

Look for excessive oil on top of the aft keel.

Close cowl flaps and note cowl flap control linkage rig, the rod to the cowl flap should split the cross shaft hole with cowl flaps closed.

Note engine breather pipe for condition and proper installation.

Check cowl flaps for clearance with exhaust tail pipe.

Physically move the exhaust tail pipe and check for some movement.

Check exhaust tail pipe for clearance with keel.

Look up tail pipe and check for condition of flame cone in muffler.

Check tail pipe support bracket for condition and wear. Check the support brackets that rivet to the fire wall for security.

Check the firewall for open holes or holes filled with putty.

Look at oil and fuel rubber or metal lines for condition and clearance or signs of chafing.

Look at the engine left-hand lower crankcase, just forward of the accessory section.

Check area of oil return line.

Check cylinder hold-down lugs for security.

Cylinder base for oil leaks.

Check oil pan gasket for oil leaks.

Check cylinder barrels for oil leaks that would result from a cracked cylinder wall.

Inspect lower cylinder at juncture of head and barrel.

Check around spark plug base in the cylinder for cracks.

Check push rod seals for leaking.

Look for excess oil on forward keel that would denote oil leak in the forward lower engine.

Check muffler shell for signs of excessive exhaust residue and if present, suggest that the heater body be checked for cracks.

Check exhaust manifold ball joint for undue stiffness, the spring loaded bolts may be too tight.

Check individual stacks for possible cracks.

Exhaust stack gaskets for condition.

Exhaust mounting flange nuts for security.

Check left side keel for condition.

Left-hand engine mounts and mount rubber bushings for security and condition.

Operate mixture control for travel and freedom of movement.

Check metering valve for fuel leaks and fuel filter cap in metering valve for security and fuel leakage.

Check propeller governor for oil leaks and proper travel of the arm.

Left-hand cowl door for excessive wear and suggest modification when needed.

Check rubber baffling and oil cooler for condition and for signs of an oil leak.

The alternate air door for proper spring tension and hinge for wear.

Now move around to the right side of the engine and make the same checks of the exhaust system and cylinders as performed on the left engine bank.

Note shower of spark for security.

Check brake fluid reservoir for condition and leaks.

Check cowl flap for condition and fit.

Hinges for wear.

Actuate the throttle and check for proper travel limits.

Check throttle arm and metering arm for unison of movement of the throttle shaft.

Check throttle shaft bushings and metering linkage for excessive wear.

Check metering valve for signs of fuel leakage.

Check side keel and lower right-hand nose bug for possible cracks.

Then ask the owner when the alternator bearings were checked last. On the IO-520 Series engine, they should be checked every 400 hours.

Inspect the upper and lower crankcase for cracks.

Thru-bolts for oil leaks.

Check engine mounts.

Push-rod seals and everything checked on left-hand engine bank.

Check cowl door latch or dzus fasteners for operation and condition.

If the engine was the IO-470 Series, make the same basic engine inspections as on the IO-520 Series, except check the alternator belt for condition and adjustment and the pulleys for alignment.

The alternator mounting lugs for cracks and security.

If the engine uses a wet vacuum pump, inspect the oil air separator for cracks.

The oil return lines to the engine.

If the engine is either the E-185-8 or E-185-11 or E-225-8, pay particular attention to exhaust stack gaskets.

Look for separation between cylinder heads and barrels.

Ask the owner if the Thompson engine driven fuel pump has been checked within the last 300 hours.

Check the bottom aft end of the magnetos.

Bottom aft ends of the starter and generator for oil that indicates shaft seal leaks.

Check the battery drain tube for condition and proper position.

Inspect the throttle arm and shaft for limit of travel.

The alternate air door for correct spring tension.

Check for wear in the door hinge and hinge wire.

Check the induction air hose.

The induction air filter for condition and security.

Check the carburetor mixture control for travel and for sticking.

This series engine has built-in oil leaks so unless they are heavy leaks, don't be concerned.

Rubber engine mounts on "E" Series engines will sag, if they sag too much, the engine sump will wear a hole in the keel. The rubber mounts can be rotated to correct the problem.

Rubber baffling is prone to tear - check for condition and security.

Look for fuel leaks around the carburetor.

The condition of fuel and oil line hose.

The "E" Series engine used the Beech Model 215 electric propeller. Check the spinner for security.

Look for cracks around the doubler in the forward point of the spinner.

Look for fore and aft movement at the blade tip.

Look at the rear spinner bulkhead for cracks.

Check the pitch change gears.

The motor gear box assembly mount grommets for wear.

The motor support bracket will sometimes crack, actuate the motor and note speed and sound.

Check blades for condition.

Look at forward cowl door hinge for condition and wear.

With the airplane on jacks, check nose gear for piston wear.

If axle will move fore and aft 3/8 inch, squawk for barrel bearing wear.

Rotate strut, note resistance to turn.

If the strut turns hard, check bolt torque on the shimmy dampener clevis bolt and on shimmy dampener attach bolt.

If bolt tension is good, check for bent shimmy dampener piston shaft.

To check for a bent shimmy dampener shaft, remove the bolt from the clevis end of the shimmy dampener piston rod and move the piston rod fore and aft. If the rod binds, it is bent.

Check for shimmy dampener fluid reservoir level inside the piston rod by inserting a wire in the aft end of the piston (might have to spread the cotter key to do this). If the wire will insert 3-1/16 inches, the reservoir is empty; if it inserts 2-3/16 inches, it is full.

Go to the cockpit, pull the landing gear circuit breaker and check the emergency hand crank casting for proper angle of attachment.

Then engage and turn the emergency hand crank counterclockwise; it should rotate 1/8 to 1/4 turn before the sector gear inside the landing gear gear box hits the internal stop.

If there is no travel, note that the landing gear motor dynamic brake is not working.

Retract the landing gear with the emergency hand crank, count the crank turns and stop after 20 turns.

This will open the landing gear doors but will not load the landing gear retract system.

Check the nose wheel bearing for tension and smooth running.

Listen, if it needs grease or if the bearings are rough, you can hear them.

Move the strut from side to side and watch the strut hinge bolts; if they move, they are loose.

Push aft on the partially retracted strut and watch strut hinge bolts, if they rotate with the strut, they are loose.

Push aft on the nose strut and check for wear in lift leg attach bushing at the strut.

In the retract rod hinge bolts in the keel.

Rock the nose gear fore and aft and look for excessive play in the retract rod.

Check rod end bearing at the idler arm location. If play is noted, investigate further because rod end may be stretched or broken.

Inspect the nose gear actuator rod boot at the firewall for condition.

Push aft on the nose strut.

Check the right-hand nose gear lift leg hinge bolt. If the hinge bolt moves up and down, bolt tension is loose or its bushing is worn.

Check for cracks in the tab on the lift leg that actuates the nose gear doors.

Check the cross pin for wear.

Check the tab base for possible cracks.

Check the nose gear door hinges, door actuating rods for bend and wear.

The cowl door actuator rods for wear and security.

Reach up in the wheel well and actuate the nose gear door actuator that turns on the cowl flap cross shaft in the keel. This shaft should move freely and its spring should snap the shaft back in a positive manner.

If the nose gear jams up in the nose gear doors during gear retraction, it is the cross shaft just mentioned that is bent or binding or its spring is broken.

Move on to the left wing and wheel well.

Look for fuel stains along the bottom front spar, around the front lower spar bathtub fitting.

Look for fuel stains along the bottom wing root fairing.

Note the fuel vents position 1-3/4 inch extension and it should point forward 10 degrees.

Later models S35 and after, have ice-free fuel vents.

Look for fuel stains around vents. If present, check the siphon break vent hole in the bottom wing just outboard of the fuel tank end.

Talk with the owner about fuel siphoning.

On the J,K and M models, talk with the owner about fuel feed-down from auxiliary fuel tanks, if he has had trouble, talk about fuel check valves in the system.

Look the wheel well area over for fuel stains, chafing fuel lines and electrical wires.

Rotate wheel, look for bearing looseness.

Check brake disc for condition and warpage.

If Goodyear brakes, check brake clips or look for hydraulic brake leaks at caliper.

Check for condition of brake hose at strut to caliper.

Check for fluid leak at strut piston.

Check for lower barrel bushing and torque knee bushing wear.

Lift strut and observe main gear strut hinge bolt security. If the bolt turns with the strut, bolt tension is loose. If the bolt moves up and down, the bushing is worn.

Lift the strut and observe the brake hose at the front strut hinge bolt position. If the hose flexes at the hose ferrul end, it will cause the hose to fail; suggest the fitting position be changed.

Check the main gear door linkage self-align bearings, the linkage should rotate.

Check uplock block for signs of contact with roller.

The uplock block cable for condition, the uplock block hinge bolt and holes for wear.

The uplock block spring for stretch and rust.

The uplock boot for correct position and condition.

Check the main gear actuator rod. The slip joint in the rod should move freely as the landing gear is lifted. If it chatters or squeaks, it should be lubricated.

With the landing gear retracted, as they are, try to rotate the main gear actuator rod. It should have some rotation.

On the V35B and after, check the landing gear squat switch cover for condition.

Move to the right wheel well and look for the same things including the condition of the tire and the landing gear squat switch cover.

Position the landing gear switch to the retract position and when the landing gear is clear, push in on the landing gear circuit breaker.

Watch the gear retract, paying particular attention to retract speed and listening to the landing gear gear-box for unusual noises.

Listen for any strange noises in the retract system.

Check all doors for proper closing.

If the right-hand inboard door hangs open, squawk the landing gear motor for low power.

If retract time is slow, squawk for high resistance in the landing gear motor electrical circuit.

Check the emergency hand crank for 1/8 to 1/4 turn before the gear hits its internal stop.

Retract and secure the emergency hand crank handle.

Check for warning horn operation.

On the Model V35B and after, pay particular attention to the emergency hand crank cover. It is possible to install the center section spar cover over the emergency hand crank cover, making it impossible to remove the cover. Now extend the landing gear electrically.

While inside the plane, look for oil stains on the carpet below the emergency hand crank. If oil is present, squawk the oil level in the landing gear gear-box.

Check the top surface of the master brake cylinders for hydraulic fluid.

Tighten the Philips head screws in the control knobs of the throttle mixture and prop controls.

Pull back on the elevator control, checking for free movement and side play.

Rotate the control wheel, looking for too-tight a chain inside the control arm. You can feel each chain link as it passes over each sprocket tooth if the chain is too tight. Then level the control wheel and note if the aileron inboard trailing edge is aligned with the outboard flap trailing edge.

Leave the cabin and move to the left wing leading edge.

Check top and bottom wing for condition.

Flip the stall warning for proper operation.

Check for pitot heat.

Check the left-hand fuel cap for signs of fuel leaks.

The left-hand wing tip and clearance light for condition.

If the wing includes tip tanks, check the outboard wing skins for distortion.

The tank for condition and leaks.

Check the left-hand aileron for freedom of movement.

Check the gap between the aileron and wing trailing edge. The gap should be the same. If the gap is wider at either end, chances are that the aileron is installed wrong.

Deflect the aileron against its down-travel stop; it should hit the stop in the wing before it hits the stop on the control column.

With aileron against the stop, strike the trailing edge with the fist, listening for a rattle noise that would indicate loose counterweights.

Check flap looseness at the trailing edge. If there is movement, go to the right-hand flap; if there is no free movement there, squawk the flap adjustment. The right flap is a slave to the left flap, so you don't want the right flap to stop before the left.

Go back to the left flap and extend the flap halfway.

Lift on the flap trailing edge and at the same time inspect the flap actuator for up-and-down movement that would indicate flap actuator wear.

At the same time look for oil leakage along the actuator piston that would indicate the need for lubricant.

Continue to extend the flap, observing the flap rollers. The flange on both rollers should be inside like the flange on a railroad car wheel.

Check limit switches for alignment and security.

Inspect flap skins for condition and especially so, where the flap actuator attaches to the flap—any deformation indicates a broken bulkhead inside the flap.

Check the pitot-static button for obstructions.

Inspect inside the aft fuselage and the differential controls on the "V" tail or the bell crank hinge bolt if 33 or 36 Models, paying particular attention to the stabilizer attach bulkhead in the fuselage for distortion and cracks and especially so on Model 35 and A35 Series.

Check control cables for condition and correct routing.

Check elevator push-pull rods for service bulletin compliance.

Rotate both push-pull rods. They should have some rotation.

Inspect both the "V" tail and the straight tail stabilizers for skin distortion at both spar root ends.

Check fuselage skins in the stabilizer area and the elevator or ruddervator skins for condition and distortion.

On the "V" tail, check the actuator arms on the ruddervator root end for security of attachment and for cracks.

Check the inboard ruddervator hinge bearing for wear and end play.

Check outboard hinge bearing for wear and visually check the counterweight for security.

Check the trim tab hinge for security and proper hinge rig.

On the A35 thru the G35, check for tab contour on the bottom.

Check for proper hinge installation and clevis bolt tension at trim tab horn, paying particular attention to the exposed tab cable for rust.

On the 33 and 36 Series, check for hinge bearing wear.

Check trim tab actuator linkage for accumulated wear.

Check actuator castings for security to the control surface and cracks.

Check the rudder spar and bell crank welds for cracks and rust.

Note the position of the fixed trim tab.

Note the condition of paint on elevator skins. If paint is heavy, question the owner about elevator balance.

Move on around the fuselage, checking static button.

Check step.

On retractable steps, check for operation as landing gear retracts.

On fixed steps, press down on step and look for skin deflection in the fuselage skin above the step attach point. If deflection is present, squawk a cracked support bulkhead in the fuselage belly.

Check the right flap.

Flap actuator and rollers.

Same as the left flap.

Check both flap travel stops for security and condition.

Retract the flaps and listen to the flap drive motor for strange sounds.

Ask the owner about cabin door problems and air leaks.

Close and latch the cabin door.

Check pressure to actuate the inside door handle, as the top latch breaks over the cam lock.

Check cabin door hinge pins for wear.

Check right-hand aileron same as left.

Note condition of the windshield.

Check all the side windows for condition and air leaks.

Check rotating beacon bulbs, strobes and landing lights for operation.

Give the owner the inspection sheet and go over the discrepancies.

AND THAT IS IT!

AIRPLANE MODEL CHANGES · BONANZA

The following are major changes between models. Performance, gross weight, cosmetic and paperwork changes are not mentioned.

1947 · 1948	D-1 thru D-40: Had fabric control surfaces.
	D-41: Magnesium control surfaces started.
	D-538: 20-gallon fuel tank optional.
	D-1078: Flap gap doors added.
	D-1225 and after: Engine primer optional.
1949	D-1823 thru D-1950 and after: E-80 starter.
A35	D-1875: Fuel boost pump optional.
	D-1581: Electric propeller governor.
1950	Landing gear retract time cut from 11.5 to 9.9
B35	seconds.
	Landing gear extension time cut from 9 to 7.4
	seconds.
	Flap travel extended to 30 degrees.
	Flap extension time cut from 17 to 11.2 seconds.
	Flap retraction time cut from 12.5 to 7.2 seconds.
1951 · 1952	More power with the E-185-11 engine.
C35	Metal propeller - 215.
	Cord width, angle of incidence of V-tail changed
	from 30 to 33 degrees.
	Wing root fillets, lowered stall speed 1 MPH.
	Improved cabin ventilation and heat.
1953	Reclining seats.
D35	36-E14 starter.
1954	E-225-8 engine optional.
E35	Two 20-gallon fuel tanks standard.
	Two 10-gallon fuel tanks optional.
	84-inch propeller.
	Aileron trimmer.
	Aluminum flaps.
	Rivets replace spot welds.
	D-3990: beefed-up wing rear spar cap.

1955	E-225-8 optional.
F35	Small third window.
	Wing spar web to tip.
	Wing leading edge skin thickness increased.
	Stabilizer spar area increased.
	Landing gear door attach points beefed up.
	Optional 10-gallon auxilary tanks.

1956	Weight increased 164 pounds.
G35	Optional 50-amp generator.
	Longer exhaust tail pipes.
	Rotating beacon optional.
	Wing structure beefed up.
	Improved cabin heat 20 percent.
	Re-designed nose strut.
	Oil/air separator.

1957	0-470-G wet sump engine.
H35	278-100 propeller.
	Automatic carburetor.
	91 - 96 octane fuel.
	Wing spar beefed up with more spar cap material.
	Wing web extended to wing tip.
	Rear spar beefed up.
	Nose keel beefed up.
	Center section beefed up.
	Thicker fuselage skins.
	Stabilizer spars beefed up.
	Rib and stiffener added to the stabilizer.
	Spar gusset gage increased.
	Elevator beefed up with intermediate inboard and outboard spar.
	Tab hinge changed.
	Tab skin gage increased.
	Elevator bungee spring tension increased.
	Dynafocal engine mounts.
	Electric primer to all cylinders.
	Gas fuel caps.
	Heavy duty Delco-Remy starter.
	D-4866 thru D-5120 and after: Improved engine mounts.
	Heavier forward belly skin.
	Ice-free hole in fuel vent.

1958	Fuel injection.
J35	IO-470-C: 250 HP engine.
	82 inch propeller (278-100).
	Electric auxilary fuel pump.
	Vernier fuel mixture.
	Auto pilot optional,factory installed.
	Louvered side cowl plates.
	Nose gear doors extended.
	Rudder travel increased.
	Optional dual beacons.

| 1959 | Rudder travel increased. |
| K35 | |

1960	No change.
M35	Debonair introduced.
33	

1961	New long rear window.
N35	IO-470-N: 260 HP engine.
	Slight decay in performance.
	Fuel capacity increased to 80 gallons.
	Landing and taxi lights moved to nose strut and nose bug.
	Shower of sparks ignition.
	Starter and magneto switches combined.
	Baggage space increased from 16.5 to 22.4 cubic feet.
	Heavy duty Delco-Remy starter.
	D-6586: Ailerons changed to aluminum.
	Retractable overhead air scoop.
	One key to operate all locks.
	Stabilizer angle of incidence changed.
	Evaporator cooler.
	Fixed entrance step.

1962 - 1963	Instrument panel changed.
P35	Piano keyboard switches abandoned.
	Optional post lights.
	Trim tab indicator.
	Rudder pedal length extended.
	Visual fuel sight tabs added to fuel tanks.
	Alternate air door ice breaker added.
	D-7127: Flottorp propeller.
	D-7239: McCauley propeller.

1964 - 1965	Structually the same as P35.
S35	IO-520-B engine.
	Cabin length extended 19 inches.
	Baggage compartment increased to 33.5 cubic feet.
	Engine canted 2½ degrees to the right and 2 degrees down.
	70 amp generator.
	Over voltage relay.
	Solid state voltage regulator.
	Increased cabin heat.
	New wing tips.
	New tail cone.
	Elevator balance horns changed.
	Long spinner.
	Optional 3 blade propeller.
	Magic hand.
	Recessed fuel vents (ice free).
	Bendix 1200 series magnetos.
	Optional large cargo door.
	Floor structure beefed up for optional fifth and sixth seats, even if seats were not called out.

1966 - 1967	First turbocharger offered.
V35-V35TC	Rear mounted fresh air scoop.
	One piece windshield.
	Improved cabin heater.
	Flap position indicator.
	McCauley, light weight, 3-bladed propeller.
	Improved dry air pump.
	Optional heated propeller de-icer (2 bladed only).

1968 - 1969	Debonair changed to Bonanza in 1968.
V35A	Long slope windshield.
	Slick magnetos replace Bendix.
	Optional elevator trim.
	D-8785: Third latch point added to the door.

36	Fuselage stretched 10 inches - first of a long line to follow.
1970 - 1972	Baffles in fuel cells.
V35B	Cleveland wheels and brakes.
V35BTC	D-9257: Removed mechanical indicator.
	D-9274: Removed nose wheel scraper.
	D-9278: Crankshaft counterweight damper pins changed from fifth to sixth order.

1984	A new instrument panel.
A36	Did away with center control column with throw over
B36TC	arm.
58 Baron	New panel has dual controls coming directly out of the panel.
	This new panel is used on the Model A36 starting with Serial E-2109 prototype.
	It is used in production starting with E-2111.
	The model 58 prototype was Serial TH-1389 and production Model started with Serial TH-1396.

1984	As of this writing, it would appear that Serial
35 Series	D-10403 will be the last of Model 35 series except on special orders. SAD!

MODEL CHANGES - DEBONAIR

1960	Serial CD-1 thru CD-250.
33	IO-470-J engine.
(233 Built)	Hartzell propeller.
	Similar to M35 Bonanza.

1961	IO-470-K engine.
A33	Retractable overhead air scoop.
(154 Built)	Heavier nose gear at CD-371 and after.
	Flottorp propeller.

1962-1964	N35 Bonanza wing leading edge.
B33	40 gallon fuel tanks, total capacity 80 gallons.
(414 Built)	Model P35 Bonanza instrument panel.
	Fillet added to vertical fin.
	Landing gear extension speed increased to 165 MPH.
	Stall warning horn.
	Adjustable front seats.
	Fuel sight tabs added to tank filler necks starting with CD-514.
	Landing light moved from nose strut to nose cowl.
	Thicker baggage door, CD-659 and after.
	Alternate air door control, CD-662 and after.

1965-1967 C33 (305 Built)	Dorsal fin. Both front and rear seats adjustable. Slight decrease in performance over B33. Improved heat for rear seat. Larger capacity heater. Right-hand wing root fresh air vent. Ice free fuel vents, CD-888 and after. Emergency static air source. 50 AMP alternator, CD-910 and after. One piece windshield. Fresh air scoop moved to dorsal fin. Flap position indicator gage. Dry vacuum pump, CD-1073 and after. Goodyear multi-disc brakes.
1966-1967 C33A (179 Built)	IO-520-B engine, 285 HP. Included most changes made to C33. Light weight three blade McCauley propeller, CE-64 and after.
1968-1969 E33 (116 Built)	Changed name to Bonanza. IO-470-K engine, 225 HP. Changes made same as V35A Bonanza. Third latch point in cabin door, CD-1171 and after. Rear cabin exhaust air scoop. Landing gear extension speed increased to 175 MPH.,starting with CD-1200 and after.
1968-1969 E33A (79 Built)	IO-520 engine. Performance same as C33A. Long slope windshield. Polished spinner. Taxi light made steerable. Slick magnetos. Gear extension speed 175 MPH. Flap speed increase, CJ-14 and after. Heat and ventilation system improved, CJ-14 and after. Fuel baffles added to fuel tanks.

139

1968-1969	225 HP aerobatic (none sold)
E33B	228 HP aerobatic (25 sold).
E33C	Aft fuselage beefed up.
	Queen Air ailerons.
	Horizontal stabilizer spars beefed up.
	Vertical fin, heavier leading edge.
	Beefed up spar stubs.
	Rudder rivets closer together.
	Heavier rudder cables.
	Aerobatic fuel boost pump.
	Quick removable front seat cushions.
1970	Start with CD-1235.
F33	IO-470-K engine 225 HP.
(20 Built)	3 light down indicator system.
	Quick cowl door release.
	Third window shape changed.
	Thicker pilot's side window with new storm window.
	High capacity instrument air pump, 432CW.
	Relay added to landing gear motor.
1970-1971	Same as Model E33A with IO-520 engine 285 HP
F33A	(1970).
(60 Built)	Cabin length same as V35B. This increased baggage compartment length 19 inches (1971).
	High capacity 232CW pressure pump.
	Cleveland wheels and brakes.
	Relay added to landing gear.
	Improved cowl door latch.
	Nose gear position indicator removed.
	Nose wheel scraper removed.
	Engine crankshaft counter weight pin changed.
	Engine designation changed to IO-520-BA.

Conclusion

My plan in writing this book,
Was to give you pilots a look

At things I've learned thru the years
And help qualm some of your fears

To show you some tips and a better way
To save your money and also your day.

May you fly your plane with care
And take God with you in the air.

Mullin Colins

Notes

Notes

Notes